COMMUNICATION SKILLS TRAINING

The Ultimate Guide for Public Speaking and Conversation, Persuasion Relationship, Workplace, Interviews. Effective Communication for Business Professional and Nonviolent

Updated Version 2nd Edition

Author: G. S. Hook

G.S.Hook Copyright © 2021

TABLE OF CONTENTS

INTRODUCTION

Communication is the transfer of information from a sender to a receiver, which must be able to understand it.

Communication serves four main functions within a group or organization: control, motivation, emotional expression, and information.

Communication acts to control individual behavior in various ways.

The communication that takes place within the group is the fundamental mechanism by which members show their frustrations and satisfaction. Communication, therefore, provides relief for the emotional expression of feelings and the fulfillment of social needs.

The final function that communication develops is related to its role as facilitator of decision-making. It provides the information that individuals and groups need to make decisions by conveying the information to identify and evaluate alternative options.

For groups to function effectively, they need to maintain some form of control over members, stimulate performance, provide a means of emotional expression, and make decisions.

Knowing that the fundamental function of language is to allow communication with peers and that not only information is transmitted in an objective way, but also orders, doubts, desires and needs are transmitted. It must be remembered that some types of speech are intended to serve two, or perhaps three, language functions simultaneously. In such cases, each aspect or function of a passage should be judged by its proper judgment. In the next job We will explain the functions of language and how they are classified, defining each one of them, knowing of course and directly how to communicate information. The functions of language are to transmit information in a direct or indirect way, transmitting of course our desires or needs.

Communication has become in today's world a transversal axis of all fields of knowledge and, at the same time, in a specific field that demands, in turn, intra and transdisciplinary visions. The new technologies produce, in the world and in societies, profound cultural mutations that must be considered; immense changes in daily life, in the ways of living and in the way of generating political decisions, appropriations of highly differentiated technologies in the world and in the society.

Communication can be understood as a process or a flow. The problems of communication occur when there are deviations or obstacles in the flow.

For communication to take place, a purpose is necessary, expressed as a message to convey. This passes through a source (the transmitter) and a receiver. The message is encoded (converted into a symbolic form) and then sent through some means (channel) to the receiver, who translates again (decodes) the message originated by the source. The result is a transfer of meaning from one person to another.

Four conditions have been described that affect the encoding of the message: skill, attitude, knowledge, and system. sociocultural.

The message is the encoding source's actual physical output. "When we talk, the message is the voice." The code or group of symbols that we use to express the meaning, the content of the message, and the decisions we make in choosing and organizing both the encoding and the content all influence our message when we write.

The Channels are the medium through which messages pass. It's up to the source to choose it and decide which channels are formal and which are informal. Formal channels are established by the organization to send messages about activities related to the work of its members. They traditionally follow a network of authorities within the organization. Other forms of messages, such as personal or social, follow informal channels within the organization.

The receiver is the object to whom the message is addressed. But before the message can be received, its symbols must be translated into a form that the recipient can understand. This is the decoding of the message. Just as the encoder was limited by his abilities, his attitudes, his knowledge and his sociocultural system, the receiver is equally restricted.

The last link in the communication process is the feedback loop. "If a communication source decodes the message it encoded, if the message is put back into the system, feedback arises." Feedback consists of verifying if we were successful in transferring our messages as we tried to transfer them from the beginning. Determine whether the understanding has been achieved or not.

Only when the receiver understands the sender's message in the terms in which he wished to convey it is communication efficient. Cultural differences, communication methods, language, and differences in each person's expectations all conspire against effective communication.

A true communication is achieved if we are interested in the language of the other person, in such a way that it can be expressed freely and sincerely, if we listen carefully and observe with conscience and we are able to put ourselves in the place of the other. Only then will we be laying the foundations for good communication.

A pleasant work environment is largely determined by the good communication that is established between people.

For the human being, it is essential to enjoy harmonious human relationships. In fact, everyone knows very well how satisfying and pleasant it is to have good human relationships and the tragedy that it means in not having them.

Not having good human relationships brings many conflicts to people at work in school and even in the experience of couples.

On the other hand, efficiency, productivity in companies and institutions have as a factor of first importance the constitution of teams and people with knowledge about

Human Relations and that their application of it is excellent. This helps the well-being of a company, both economically and at the level of communication of workers because in conflictive environments and with discord, precisely the opposite happens.

Sure, but there can be no human relationships if there is no communication. Communication is the process in which various data, ideas and attitudes are transmitted and received that constitute the basis for common understanding or agreement.

In Human and Public Relations communication is essential, without it life in society would be impossible.

That is why we will study the elements and purposes of communication to learn to communicate and have better human relationships in all aspects of our lives.

CHAPTER 1

ALL BASICS OF COMMUNICATIONS

Basic communication skills, whether verbal or written, are an important part of relationship skills. This is true at home, in the workplace, and in general interactions or relationships. Whether written or verbal, the message received is far more important than the message sent.

With good communication skills, the person receiving the message understands it exactly the way the sender intended it to be understood. With poor communication, the message can easily be misunderstood or misinterpreted. In that case, the interaction could become simply a waste of time, or in a worst-case scenario, could result in severe unintended consequences if the message is acted upon incorrectly. Basic communication skills provide a foundation for good communication.

Effective communication skills include the proper use and expression of words, along with consideration of the "image" presented and a good understanding of how the message will most likely be perceived.

Basic Communication Skills - General Communication

Communication can be either written or interpersonal. Many of the basic communication skills apply to both:

Sharpen Your Listening Skills. The first and foremost thing which one can do towards improving communication skills is that make a conscious effort of listening carefully to what the other person is saying. In a professional life, whether in meetings or group discussion, it is very important to engage in active listening.

Know Your Audience. Choose your words appropriately. Using big words to impress an audience that doesn't understand any of them is probably a waste of time. Engage your audience by including topics of particular interest to them - how are they affected. As "receivers" of a message, everyone wants to feel they have some connection to that message. If they don't feel connected, the message will most likely be ignored.

Show Appropriate Level Of Respect. Everyone deserves basic respect. Profanity is rarely appreciated. Communication with the president of the company or a supervisor should be more formal than communicating with a co-worker, even if the information given is the same. Don't order people to do things. Even if compliance is mandatory, the request can be phrased in a way that conveys importance but does not instill resentment that could result in a job poorly done.

Image Should Be Clean And Neat. Letters and emails should be easy to read with no misspelled words. This is particularly important when making an initial contact. Seeing someone for the first time immediately sparks a first impression. In most cases, being clean and neat plays a large part in forming a good impression.

Dressing for Success is particularly important in preparing for an interview.

Be Clear And Concise. Don't ramble. Most people have a low tolerance for communication that is off-topic and seems never-ending. With regard to written communication, read it over several times to be sure it is exactly what you want to say. The content of written material must be very clear because, unlike verbal communication, spontaneous questioning is not possible.

Practice Empathy. One should always try to understand the other person's viewpoint which reduces misunderstanding to a great extent. Developing empathy towards others strengthens any relationship. It helps you to comprehend the unspoken aspects of the communication and respond accordingly.

Try To Be Brief, But Specific. According to the popular notion, BRIEF– Background, Reason, Information, End and Follow Up. This is followed while sending professional emails. It helps to keep the emails short but containing all vital points. This acronym can be used for verbal communication skills too. Any official communication, one should follow 7 C's of communication- Complete, Coherent, Correct, Courteous, Clear, Concise, Concrete.

Customize Your Message To Your Audience. The communication message would be different for a co-worker, or boss, or senior, or kids, or elders and so on. It is wise to gauge the other person's attitude, edit the message accordingly and then delivering it.

Avoid The Distractions. It is very unprofessional and rude to check your phone messages while another person is speaking with you. If it is not absolutely necessary to use the technology, you can avoid it for some time. If you can't avoid it, just make an effort to at least look up to that person while he is sharing something.

Make Clarifications As And When Needed. When engaging in communication with others, one should ask questions in between and avoid staring or nodding silently. It is also good to repeat the last few words of what the speaker is saying which shows your interest level. It also helps in clarifying facts that may have been wrongly interpreted. It is also a nice way to fill in awkward silences in between conversations. It helps in initiating small talks between two people, which increases their bonding.

Present A Story. Stories create a lasting impression on the audience. Stories usually activate our brain cells, make the presentation less boring, make us perform better in interviews and so on. The idea is communicated to the receiver in the form of a story which makes it interesting and attractive.

Prepare A Small Script. One should always be prepared for small talks and have a fixed plan regarding small talks. The FORD method (Family, Occupation, Recreation, Dreams) is also quite helpful in initiating small talks. The FORD method helps small talks to convert into a long conversation with meaningful sharing of information.

Avoid Unnecessary Communication Fillers. The unnecessary words in between conversations like Ah, Um, Oho, etc. disturbs the natural flow of the speech. It is better to avoid them as much as possible. Try to take a deep breath and pause in between speeches to minimize the use of communication fillers.

Make Correct Use Of Humor. Humor relaxes people and releases endorphins which help lower anxiety and stress. Most people can relate to someone who makes them laugh heartily. It is wise to be funny or witty in conversations, but do make sure that it is appropriate to the situation. The use of humor should be done in order to minimize communication barriers, gain affection as well as the trust of others.

Avoid Differentiating People. It is always advised to communicate with other people on an equal basis. In all situations, avoid talking in people's back and avoid making favorites. If you treat people equally, you can easily build trust and respect. Always verify what people have understood from your conversation in order to avoid negative feelings and confusion. Always encourage honest and open feedback from your receiver communication skills basics.

Make A Conscious Effort Of Conflict Resolution. Be prepared to resolve any issues as they arise. It is vital to be an effective negotiator. You can apply your listening skills to understand all perspective of an argument. In the process of conflict resolution, try not to be too judgmental and practice empathy communication skills basics.

Keep A Positive Attitude. People tend to avoid people who are always miserable and sulky. It is always best to maintain a cheerful, positive attitude towards life. Sometimes in life, things do not go as planned. In such cases, maintain your calm mind and communicate effectively with people. Do not forget to keep a bright smile on your face.

Do Not Interrupt. When someone is giving a speech, do not interrupt him again and again. This disrupts the natural flow of communication. So better bite your tongue and hold back. Let the other person finish his speech before you start putting your questions communication skills basics.

Try To Assert Yourself. The communication made between two more persons should be open, clear, direct, honest, and respectful. Direct and assertive expression of your ideas helps in increased self-esteem and improved decision making. One should value his own idea, accept feedbacks positively, learn how to say no and express all negative ideas in a positive way. Sometimes it is alright to be angry, but one should have a respectful approach.

Anticipate Possible Reactions And Counter Them. Whether writing a letter/email or preparing to speak to a group, anticipate questions, comments, and criticisms that might arise. You can alter or expand the information given to cover anticipated feedback. Or be prepared to counter this feedback at a later date.

Basic Communication Skills - Interpersonal Communication

Interpersonal communication is far more complicated than written in the sense that response and interaction is immediate. There is usually not time to compose the perfect response or explanation. Emotions also play a larger part in interpersonal communication. Therefore, in addition to the skills listed above, the following should also be considered basic communication skills.

Interpersonal Communication Skills Focus on Sight and Sound as well as Content:

Body Language. The image projected by the speaker and the perception received by the listener - is the most important part of interpersonal communication. In some cases, we don't even have to speak. Sometimes we can see a person across the room and immediately decide whether we want to interact with them or avoid them. First impressions can be that strong. This is especially true in a job interview. If we make a bad first impression, we may have to work very hard to overcome it.

Being able to project a positive image is a relationship skill. Generally, if we have a positive self-image, it is much easier to project a positive image to other people. And a positive image usually results in a more positive interaction. This is true in casual interactions (a store clerk), more formal interactions (boss or co-worker) and intimate relationships (family or close friends). Understanding that perception is not always reality can also help us avoid jumping to conclusions. Sometimes our projected image is misperceived and sometimes we misperceive the projected image of another person.

Gestures and symbols are also important. Someone shaking their fist at us may rightly be interpreted as someone to stay away from. The same may be true of someone with a tattoo or wearing a t-shirt that promotes violence. Lack of eye contact may send a message of insincerity or disinterest. Although it could also indicate a cultural difference or low self-esteem.

What is the best way to avoid a distorted image or perception? As mentioned earlier, developing personal strengths may help us project a more positive image. And empathy can help us avoid jumping to conclusions. Asking questions to clarify what we are thinking will also help.

Tone of Voice. A reflection of feelings - is the second-most important part of interpersonal communication. Generally, we will not listen to someone who is yelling at us, putting us down or acting better than us. All of these feelings - anger, condescension, superiority - come through loud and clear in tone of voice. In good communication, an even-toned delivery is encouraged. This is particularly true in customer service. Feelings and emotions should always be expressed in an appropriate manner, based on that specific interaction or relationship.

Content. The words and message, although listed third in interpersonal communication, are still very important. As outlined in Basic Communication Skills --

General Communication, choose words carefully and be sure the message is clear and concise.

CHAPTER 2

THE IMPORTANCE OF COMMUNICATION

Developing your communication skills can help all aspects of your life, from your professional life to social gatherings and everything in between. The ability to communicate information accurately, clearly and as intended, is a vital life skill and something that should not be overlooked. It's never too late to work on your communication skills and by doing so, you may well find that you improve your quality of life.

To demonstrate just how important good communication is, I've listed some of the benefits it can have on your professional life.

In Demand By Businesses. Oral and written communication proficiencies are consistently ranked in the top ten desirable skills by employer surveys year after year. Employees are often encouraged to take online courses and in-person training to improve their presentation and communication skills.

It Improves Team Building. Honest and effective communication can create a strong team. When staff consult with each other, consider other opinions and discuss their progress, they will be more enthused to collaborate. As a result, the strong unit that they create makes the workplace more enjoyable, and they will be eager to perform well so they don't let their teammates down. Indeed, communication helps solve employee morale issues by keeping entire teams in the loop, making all team members feel useful within the workplace. This lack of secrecy not only boosts team spirit but it also has a positive effect on staff attitudes.

It Boosts Growth. Great communication contributes to the growth of the business, which goes hand in hand with your career. It eliminates uncertainties and speeds up the process of policies to ensure there is a smooth delivery of projects. Take eCommerce website Zappos, for example; their ethos relies on great communication within the organization and with their clients – something that earned them a spot on Fortune magazine's 2015 list of the 100 best companies to work for.

Helps Your Career Progression. You will need to request information, discuss problems, give instructions, work in teams, interact with colleagues and clients. If you are to achieve co-operation and effective teamwork, good human relations skills are essential. Also, as the workplace is also becoming more global, there are many factors to consider if you are to communicate well in such a diverse environment. Being able to deliver messages clearly and understand other people means work can be completed more effectively and to the benefit of the company as a whole. Employers want staff who can think for themselves, use initiative and solve problems, staff who are interested in the long-term success of the company. If you are to be seen as a valued member of the organization, it is important not just to be able to do your job well, but also to communicate your thoughts on how the processes and products or services can be improved.

Allows You To Speak Concisely. It is natural to feel some nerves when speaking to superiors or to clients. Communication skills training will help you learn how best to communicate effectively in a wide range of situations, and how to be direct in order to get the most out of your dealings with others.

Builds Better Rapport With Customers. Customers desire nothing more than to be understood by a company and they wish to feel like they are being heard and listened to. This is a particularly important point if your business involves a large amount of contact with customers, either face-to-face or over the phone.

Influences How You Learn. Communication skills have played an important part of your existing knowledge and beliefs. You learn to speak in public by first having conversations, then by answering questions and then by expressing your opinions. You learn to write by first learning to read, then by writing and learning to think critically. Good communication skills help you absorb information and express your ideas in a clear, concise and meaningful way to other people.

Enhances Your Professional Image. You want to make a good first impression on your friends and family, instructors, and employer. They all want you to convey a positive image, as it reflects on them. In your career, you will represent your business or company in spoken and written form. Your professionalism and attention to detail will reflect positively on you and set you up for success.

It Increases Innovation. If employees are scared of communicating their thoughts and ideas out of fear of being rejected, then they are likely to become stagnant in their career and only contribute the bare minimum. However, if there is an open line of communication between supervisors and staff members, they are encouraged to be more creative and innovative within the workplace, and they are likely to put forth new and creative ideas. In today's fast-moving workplace, most ideas are likely to be pushed under the carpet due to a lack of communication. As Cisco managing director Alex Goryachev writes on Forbes: 'People listen mostly to respond rather than to understand. However, digitization demands active listening to the ecosystem in order to survive and develop collaborative strategies with startups, partners, and customers around the world'.

Managing Diversity in the Workforce. Good communication is even more important if the workforce is diverse. With a mix of races, nationalities, genders or faiths on the job, it's easy for people to accidentally offend each other. If promotion and employee review rules aren't clear, minority workers may feel they've been discriminated against. Policies that clearly spell out how the company applies rewards and penalties can clear things up. Clear guidelines telling employees how to treat each other helps avoid unwanted conflict.

It Improves Productivity. Being able to communicate effectively at work can help increase overall productivity. Managers can understand their employees' talents and skills and will then give clear directions to the people that are best suited for the job, thus increasing the overall turnaround time of any given project. For example, one colleague may be faster and better at using Excel than others; therefore, through communication, a manager can identify this and task them with managing the spreadsheets. If there was a lack of conversation, meanwhile, the project would suffer, and the entire process would slow down, negatively affecting the goal of the company, as a result.

It Increases Efficiency. Poor communication compromises efficiency, as well as the overall quality of work. When instructions aren't provided clearly, mistakes are bound to happen. On the other hand, clear instructions eliminate the need to clarify and correct any issues. Think back to a time where you didn't communicate well with a colleague. It probably resulted in wasted time, effort and resources. So, if you happen to have a manager that doesn't communicate effectively, make sure you ask the right questions to get the information that you need to successfully complete a project. Over time, they will understand what they should be supplying you with so you can start working on your tasks.

It Increases Loyalty. When you have a good line of communication with management, you're naturally going to be more loyal to the organization. You will feel comfortable discussing any professional or personal issues, and you'll be more committed to the company. This free line of communication also builds trust between a manager and an employee, which results in a loyal relationship. A two-way line of respect ensures there's no micromanagement involved and that an employee is trusted to get on with the job that they were hired to do.

It Reduces Mitigation Conflict. Two people in the workplace may feel that they are communicating well, but because they both have different methods of communication, they are misunderstanding each other. Therefore, working with different personalities requires excellent communication skills to limit any conflict in the workplace. If you are experiencing conflict at work, it's important to look beyond the issue at hand and identify the other person's thought process. You need to consider the communication pattern of the receiver to get a better understanding of what they are trying to say.

It Increases Employee Engagement. Good communication goes far beyond talking; it's more about connecting and engaging with others. When teams are engaged, they are more aligned with the company's goals and are generally more motivated to work towards the set targets. It's also easier for managers to identify what makes a positive and satisfying working environment, allowing them to work towards achieving a balanced working life for their employees.

It Resolves Problems. There's bound to be characters that clash and opinions that differ within any working environment. And what's the best way to solve those problems? Clear communication! Effective communication isn't about who's right and wrong; it's about having open, honest and positive discussions to ensure everyone's needs are met! You're not always going to see eye to eye with your work nemesis, but if you can find a way to work well with them, you'll make the environment much more enjoyable for everyone around you!

It Enhances Skills. Managers can identify hidden talents when they communicate clearly with their employees. By doing so, they can tap into these skills and help enhance them, which will contribute to the overall success of the business. For example, John may be hired as a customer service representative, but through conversation, his manager identifies that he has previous experience in marketing. John is then transferred to Marketing and is much better suited at the position. If the lack of communication were there, however, John would have become stagnant later down the line, and the business would have lost great talent.

In every aspect of your job, you'll be required to communicate in one way or other. It's important to understand just how valuable effective communication is and what impact it can have on your relationships and your progression within the working world.

CHAPTER 3

PUBLIC SPEAKING

Communications in its multiple forms pervades today's business environment. With numerous job interviews, conference calls, meetings, product presentations, workshops, and public events, more and more leaders realize the importance of developing good interpersonal communication skills within their company. Yet the majority of executives and employees continue to neglect and overlook the use of public speaking, leaving the advancements and better career opportunities for those who take proactive steps to master the art of speaking in public.

The truth is that you might have the best products or services, years of experience or an outstanding business idea, but if you do not communicate this to your target audiences, you are limiting your effectiveness. All too often, the very best and inspiring stories in organizations and companies go untold because of people's reluctance to or fear of taking the stage.

Whether your goal is to enhance your professional growth, take your business to the next level, or inspire, persuade and motivate other people to follow your lead, you will have to learn how to convey your ideas in front of a group of people in a clear, structured and captivating manner.

However, becoming an effective public speaker does not have to turn into one of the necessary, yet unpleasant goals on your professional advancement list. The art of public speaking holds many practical benefits that go far beyond delivering a project presentation or holding a successful meeting.

Developing your communication skills and learning to speak in public:

- Opens up new opportunities for career advancement
- Positions you as an authority

- Sets you apart from your competition
- Attracts the right customers to your business
- Presents technical or business information effectively
- Produces a faster sales cycle
- Allows you to effectively market your business or promote your products to larger audiences
- Improves internal communication
- Helps you to easily assume leadership and train others
- Increases employees' productivity
- Prepares you for spontaneous speaking challenges (e.g. delivering a speech at short notice)
- Establishes greater credibility and helps your clients' loyalty
- Motivates and persuades other people to reach and attain professional goals
- Makes you a desirable guest on local, regional and national conferences, seminars and public speaking events

Personal and Social Benefits of Public Speaking

A series of psychological studies conducted at Tufts University in Medford, Massachusetts, show that it takes people on average three to five seconds to form an impression about someone they meet for the first time.

Improving your ability to speak in front of others and learning to talk about who you are and what you do with natural grace and authenticity can go a long way in expanding your social circle, building strong relationships with successful, like-minded people and making new friends.

Other personal benefits of public speaking include:

- Increased self-confidence
- Improved communication skills
- Increased organizational skills
- Greater social influence
- Enhanced ability to listen
- Greater possibility of meeting new people

- Lesser anxiety and fear when speaking in front of others
- Improved memory
- Enhanced persuasion ability
- Greater control over emotions and body language

Three Styles of Speech

The three most common styles of speeches that you encounter in today's business and social world are - impromptu, manuscript and extemporaneous. To become a great public speaker you will have to learn and ace each one of them, as it will allow you to speak confidently and effectively in front of any number of listeners and in any given situation.

Impromptu speech. Impromptu speech is prompted by the occasion rather than being planned in advance. While famous public speakers often joke that best impromptu speeches should be prepared weeks in advance, usually in real life we have very little or no time to prepare before we speak in front of the audience. Some examples of impromptu speech could be your boss asking you to bring the rest of your team up to date, or a group of friends urging you to say a few words at a non-profit event.

Manuscript speech. This type of speech is written like a manuscript and is meant to be delivered word for word. Manuscript speeches are used on many political and social occasions when every word carries a lot of weight and should not be misquoted. One of the most common examples of a manuscript speech is a political figure delivering a speech that has been written by another person.

Extemporaneous speech. Extemporaneous speech is the most commonly used type of speech that helps to establish emotional connection with the audience. It is built around key points, but the material can be presented freely, allowing the speaker to make changes in their speech based on the listeners' reaction.

Let us address one of the major obstacles that most people face when it comes to speaking in front of a group of people – Fear.

Overcoming Fear of Public Speaking

An opportunity to speak in front of an audience, whether it is three or three hundred people, is the chance to sell your business or service to potential customers or clients. However, one of the biggest obstacles that many businessmen and women face is the fear of public speaking.

According to national surveys and research results, fear of public speaking (or 'glossophobia') ranks among the top dreads, surpassing the fear of heights, fear of spiders and even fear of death itself. As Jerry Seinfeld put it – "at a funeral, the average person would rather be in the casket than giving the eulogy."

So what is it that makes the fear of public speaking so strong and so debilitating? Why does 75% of population suffer from speech anxiety every time they are asked to talk in front of other people? How can we overcome the fear of speaking in public and polish our communication skills? What can we do to transform the fear of public speaking into enthusiasm and positive energy?

Psychologists know that the very fact of being in the spotlight often triggers the whole range of physical reactions that we would experience in the face of real life-threatening danger as:

- Pounding heart
- Dry mouth
- Shaky hands
- Quivering voice
- Cold sweaty palms
- Stomach cramps

Recent research conducted at University of California at Los Angeles might finally shed some light on this issue. MRI scans of the brain showed that the shock and distress of rejection activate the same part of the brain, called the anterior cingulate cortex that also responds to physical pain. Another study conducted by Edward E. Smith, director of cognitive neuroscience at Columbia University demonstrated that the feeling of rejection is one of the most painful emotions that can be sustained even longer than fear.

How can these findings explain the fear of public speaking?

If it is painful enough to be rejected by just one person, imagine the pain we could experience when being rejected by a large group of people. Of course, our emotions range from being absolutely terrified to feeling very uncomfortable. Our anxiety and fright before the speech, however, may be caused not by fear of public speaking per se' but by the audience's reaction to our performance. Or put simply, we are afraid that our nervousness will interfere with our ability to perform and we will end up embarrassing ourselves. Accepting our fear helps us to take proactive steps in addressing stage fright and letting the adrenaline rush work for you, not against you.

Two Biggest Myths about the Fear of Public Speaking

When it comes to public speaking there are two common misconceptions that many business owners and leaders fall prey to:

Myth One: Great public speaking skills are an inborn talent. Of course, some people find it easier to speak in public than the other, but the majority of successful speakers have trained themselves to perform through persistence, preparation, and practice. The bottom line is that if you can speak in front of two friends, you can deliver a presentation before an audience.

Myth Two: Fear of public speaking is negative and undesirable. This is another common misconception that holds many new speakers back. They believe that stage fright is a sign of their inadequacy and lack of public speaking skills. This could not be further away from truth. No one escapes the rush of adrenaline that accompanies a presentation in front of an audience. The difference between successful speakers and 'rookies', is that they have learned to transform and use fear to their advantage.

Fear is not only a normal reaction to a public speaking event but actually boosts our performance. Psychologists agree that some amount of fear heightens your awareness, improves your concentration, sharpens your thinking and gives you an energy boost. It is fear that allows most speakers to perform better during the actual presentation than during practice.

Ways to Transform the Public Speaking Fear into Excitement

The fear of public speaking should not turn into an obstacle to your professional and personal growth. It is much easier to build a business or to advance in your career when you are able to speak with confidence and authenticity to any size group.

If you are worried that fear may worsen instead of improve your presentation, here are 5 Practical Ways to transform it into unshakable confidence and excitement:

Deep Breathing. Such strong emotions as anxiety and fear trigger in your body very specific "fight or flight" response: your muscles tighten, your heart rate increases, your blood pressure goes up and your breathing becomes shallow. While this physical reaction may be helpful in escaping danger it is hardly helpful during the presentation (as you can neither run away from your audience nor fight with it). However, since your breathing rate is directly connected to your emotional reaction, the fastest and easiest way to take your emotions under control and regain confidence is through deep breathing. Whether you are to talk to potential clients or make a presentation to your team, make sure that you remember to breathe deeply and evenly before and during your speech.

Shifting focus outwards. Paul L. Witt, Ph.D., assistant professor of communication studies at Texas Christian University, believes that many people perform worse than they could because they focus too much on their physical symptoms (i.e. butterflies, shaky hands, sweaty palms) and on their embarrassment instead of concentrating on their breathing and their speech. This problem could be easily avoided by shifting focus from how we feel or look to the message we want to share with our audience.

Visualizing. Visualization or mental rehearsal has been routinely used by many top athletes as a part of the training for a competition. In addition to athletics, research has shown that visualization helps to improve performance in such areas as communication, public speaking, and education. To ensure that your presentation goes smoothly, aside from actual preparation and the rehearsal of your speech, take 10-15 minutes a day to relax, close your eyes and visualize the room you are speaking in, the people in the auditorium and yourself confidently delivering your speech, smiling, and moving across the stage.

Focusing On Facts, Not Fears. Instead of focusing on irrational fears (e.g. mind going blank, audience getting bored) concentrate your thoughts on positive facts such as: "I have practiced my speech many times", "I am an expert on this topic", "I have notes with major bullet points to keep the structure of my talk". Focusing on positive facts and on what you can offer takes your thoughts away from irrational scenarios about what can go wrong.

Building Your Speech On Clarity, Not Complexity. While it is often tempting to include as much useful information in your speech as possible, practice shows that this might not be a good idea. Organizing the speech or presentation around two-three main points, allows you to relax and not worry so much about running out of time or forgetting to mention something important to the listeners.

Components of a Successful Speech

Given the choice, many of us would prefer to submit a written report rather than get up and convey the same information orally. And it is not only fear of public speaking that holds us back. The written language holds many advantages. Written words can be chosen with greater deliberation and care. Written arguments can be expressed in a sophisticated, complex and lengthy manner and the readers have the option of taking in the text at a pace that is comfortable for them and even re-reading it if they choose to do so.

This degree of precision is hard to achieve when delivering a speech. The presenter does not have the same amount of time to choose the words that would best explain their opinion or idea. While the listeners have to rely only on their cognitive skills to recall and analyze the message.

On the other hand, verbal communication can be significantly more effective in expressing the meaning of the message to the audience. The speaker has an opportunity to use other means of communication that written language does not allow.

Let us take a look at the other means of communication available to speaker besides the power of the spoken word. These include:

- Storytelling
- Body language
- Tone of voice
- Pauses
- Visual Cues

Storytelling

Everyone loves to listen to stories. A well-told story has an almost hypnotic effect on the listeners. People might forget what you wore during a presentation or some of the charts, graphs and statistical data shown to them, but they will never forget the stories that you told them.

Many leaders and managers avoid storytelling in their presentations, believing that they have to keep their speech formal and business-like. This is one of the main reasons they often fail to grab their audience's attention and establish an atmosphere of trust and respect with their listeners.

In the business world whether you are speaking in front of two hundred people or making a presentation to your client, do not be afraid to include a few personal stories in your speech. Professional public speakers use storytelling in their presentations for a variety of purposes which includes to:

- Make statistical data, graphics, and facts more vivid and interesting.
- Relieve tension
- Make important points of the presentation memorable
- Establish a connection with the particular audience
- Emphasize the message
- Introduce controversial issues
- Encourage thinking
- Shape people's beliefs
- Raise the energy level of the group

- Motivate people to act

Storytelling can be defined as a structured narrative account of real or imagined events that is widely used in public speaking as a medium for sharing, interpreting and offering the content of the story to the listeners. The best stories to use in your public speech may involve true facts from your life; self-effacing humorous facts about your past mistakes, and challenges; success stories from famous people's biographies; and stories that explore the history of your business.

Not every story will grab your audience's attention and interest. There are a few important points that should be taken into consideration when choosing the right story for your speech:

Do's

- Always make your story relevant to the subject at hand
- Keep your stories simple and short
- Eliminate inconsequential detail

- Space stories at intervals to reemphasize your message
- Make sure the plot of the story involves a lesson or a transformation outcome that your listeners can relate to and benefit from.
- Use appropriate body language and facial expressions to convey emotions to your listeners.
- Use elements of the story that your audience can relate to (e.g. people, places, and familiar facts).
- Emphasize the adjectives and verbs in your stories to make them sound more interesting.
- Learn your stories by heart

Don'ts

- Do not use more than two or three stories on the same topic as each successive one will lose its impact
- Do not use terms that are foreign to the experience of the audience

- Do not fill stories with too many characters, events or details

Tone Of Voice

A speaker's confidence, emotional state, and attitude is often revealed in the tone of voice. In the area of public speaking your voice becomes a powerful instrument that allows you to engage, charm and encourage your audience to listen.

It may mean that people are more influenced by the sound and quality of an individual's voice than by its content. Of course, these findings do not imply that the weight of the spoken words should be ignored or that it diminishes. They, however, demonstrate that the effect of vocal cues on your listeners have to be taken into consideration when preparing your speech and delivering it in public. In order to better grasp the impact that your voice has on an audience try to recall a public speaker or an old University professor who talked in a monotone voice.

How difficult was it to keep your focus on what was being said?

Speakers who talk in a tone with no variations, which usually happens when a public speaker is reading the speech or recalling it verbatim, quickly lose their audience's attention and even put some of their listeners to sleep. To avoid people dozing off or daydreaming during your presentation you have to learn to control your tone of voice and use it to make your speech more expressive and hypnotizing.

Pitch

Pitch is a placement of voice on the musical scale ranging from high to low. Usually, men speak in a lower pitch (about 120 Hz) than women (220 Hz).

Research shows that low-pitch speaking voices, both for men and women are preferable to the listeners as they are associated with authority, credibility, strength, and self-confidence. A great example of a low-pitch speaking voice is that of American actor James Earl Jones. Many remember him as the voice of Darth Vader in Star Wars and Simba's dad in The Lion King.

High-pitched voices, on the contrary, are less pleasant to the ears of the audience as they are perceived as less persuasive, weaker, less truthful and more nervous. Partly, this unconscious assumption holds true, as the nervousness of a speaker is often reflected in a high-pitched, "thin" or nasal sounding voice or in the habit of raising the pitch at the beginning or end of the phrase.

While there are no "golden" voice standard to fit all, voice coaches usually suggest public speakers talk at the lower end of their speaking voice to make it sound more rich and expressive.

The Power of Pause

As strange as it may seem to many executives and business leaders, who are accustomed to persuading and managing other people - public speaking is not just about talking in public.

In most cases there is no need to fill the silence with meaningless words such as "uhm", "like", and "you know". Doing this only distracts the audience from what is being said and gives the impression of nervousness and lack of clarity.

Accomplished speakers are aware of this and often use the power of pause to:

- Raise the impact of a remark
- Bridge ideas
- Underline the last thing that was said
- Create anticipation for the next remark
- Instill more humor and passion into the presentation
- Give time for the listeners to absorb the information
- Leave the room for reflection after questions

Visual Aids

They often say that a picture is worth a thousand words. Adding a visual dimension to your presentation can make it look more vivid, graphic and professional-looking. Although, not every business presentation or public speaking event should forcedly be accompanied by slide shows, graphs, and pictures. Lincoln's Gettysburg Address is a mere 269 words long, but it would take over 2000 pictures to transmit the same message to the audience.

When planning your public speech or your presentation you should always keep your main objective in mind.

- What is the purpose of your speech?
- What is it that you want to achieve with your performance?
- What do you want your listeners to take from your presentation?

Is your goal to motivate, empower or persuade your audience to take action? In this case, you might not need to use visual aids, as your listeners already know what they should be doing. Slides of explanations, charts, graphs, and pictures will not add any value to the presentation. On the contrary, doing too may actually interfere with the momentum and weaken the emotional connection established by the speaker with the audience.

On the other hand, if your goal is to help your listeners understand and remember some key points of your presentation, there is no doubt that you can benefit enormously from including some visual elements and data in your presentation.

CHAPTER 4

Aggressive, Assertive, Submissive Communications Skills

What Is Aggressive Communication?

During aggressive communication, you stand up for yourself in a way that is inappropriate and may violate the rights of others. You may find that people seem exhausted, overwhelmed or drained after talking with you when you are in an aggressive state. Some people also establish their superiority through aggressive communication by putting others down.

We've all dealt with aggressiveness as a communication style in our relationships at one time or another, whether it's come from a parent, a friend, a co-worker, or a romantic partner. In fact, if this style of communication was common in your family as you were growing up, it may be a style of communication that you use without realizing it. Aggressiveness is a mode of communication and behavior where one expresses their feelings, needs, and rights without regard or respect for the needs, rights, and feelings of others. This style of communication is favored by narcissists and bullies, but it can show up in conversations anywhere, from the office to the bedroom. When aggressive communication is used by one person, emotional force is often experienced so that the rights of others are not even allowed to surface. When this happens, others feel victimized and relationships suffer. In that way, relationship aggression is bad for the aggressors as well as the recipients of the aggression.

Why It's Harmful

In the moment, aggressive communication can feel very satisfying, particularly if you have social anxiety and are used to not speaking up. You may get your way by bullying others and it may give you a sense of power and control. If you lack this feeling in your life, you may become addicted to it through aggressive communication.

However, aggressive communication is likely to result in the development of enemies and hurt relationships with loved ones. After you have hurt someone you care about, you may feel shame or guilt. This can also inhibit your social skills and make future social situations much more difficult for you. In this way, communicating aggressively becomes a vicious cycle from which you cannot escape.

The toll that relationship conflict takes in terms of stress can affect us in many ways. It can impact our stress levels, and it can also affect our health and happiness. Because of the lack of real connection in their relationships, aggressive individuals tend to cause others stress and experience increased levels of stress themselves, as their relationships tend to be conflicted and their personal goals not as often achieved. A powerful tool to use in the face of aggressive communication is assertiveness. Assertiveness is often used as a synonym for forceful communication but, in contrast to aggressiveness, assertiveness involves expressing one's own needs and rights while respecting the needs and rights of others and maintaining the dignity of both parties. This results in healthier relationships and increased life satisfaction. And while communication styles aren't the only way that aggressiveness can surface in relationships, those who endeavor to change their aggressive communication patterns to assertive ones tend to be open to other improvements as well.

Aggressive communicators will often:

- Try to dominate others
- Use humiliation to control others
- Criticize, blame, or attack others
- Be very impulsive
- Have low frustration tolerance
- Speak in a loud, demanding, and overbearing voice
- Act threateningly and rudely
- Not listen well
- Interrupt frequently
- Use "you" statements

The aggressive communicator will say, believe, or behave like:

- "I'm superior and right and you're inferior and wrong."
- "I'm loud, bossy and pushy."
- "I can dominate and intimidate you."
- "I can violate your rights."
- "I'll get my way no matter what."
- "You're not worth anything."
- "It's all your fault."
- "I react instantly."
- "I'm entitled."
- "You owe me."
- "I own you."

What Is Assertiveness?

It's not always easy to identify truly assertive behavior. This is because there's a fine line between assertiveness and aggression, and people can often confuse the two. For this reason, it's useful to define the two behaviors so that we can clearly separate them:

Assertiveness is based on balance. It requires being forthright about your wants and needs, while still considering the rights, needs and wants of others. When you're assertive, you are self-assured and draw power from this to get your point across firmly, fairly and with empathy.

Aggressive behavior is based on winning. You do what is in your own best interest without regard for the rights, needs, feelings, or desires of other people. When you're aggressive, the power you use is selfish. You may come across as pushy or even bullying. You take what you want, often without asking.

So, a boss who places a pile of work on your desk the afternoon before you go on vacation, and demands that it gets done straight away, is being aggressive. The work needs to be done but, by dumping it on you at an inappropriate time, he or she disregards your needs and feelings.

When you, on the other hand, inform your boss that the work will be done but only after you return from vacation, you hit the sweet spot between passivity (not being assertive enough) and aggression (being hostile, angry or rude). You assert your own rights while recognizing your boss's need to get the job done.

Assertive behavior may not be appropriate in all workplaces. Some organizational and national cultures may prefer people to be passive and may view assertive behavior as rude or even offensive. Research has also suggested that gender can have a bearing on how assertive behavior is perceived, with men more likely to be rewarded for being assertive than women. So, it pays to consider the context in which you work before you start changing your behavior.

The Benefits of Being Assertive

One of the main benefits of being assertive is that it can help you to become more self-confident, as you gain a better understanding of who you are and the value that you offer. Assertiveness provides several other benefits that can help you both in your workplace and in other areas of your life. In general, assertive people:

- **Make great managers.** They get things done by treating people with fairness and respect and are treated by others the same way in return. This means that they are often well-liked and seen as leaders that people want to work with.
- **Negotiate successful "win-win" solutions.** They are able to recognize the value of their opponent's position and can quickly find common ground with him.
- Are better doers and problem solvers. They feel empowered to do whatever it takes to find the best solution to the problems that they encounter.
- **Are less anxious and stressed.** They are self-assured and don't feel threatened or victimized when things don't go as planned or as expected.

How to Become More Assertive

It's not easy to become more assertive, but it is possible. So, if your disposition tends to be more passive or aggressive, then it's a good idea to work on the following areas to help you to get the balance right:

1. Value Yourself and Your Rights

To be more assertive, you need to gain a good understanding of yourself, as well as a strong belief in your inherent value and your value to your organization and team.

This self-belief is the basis of self-confidence and assertive behavior. It will help you to recognize that you deserve to be treated with dignity and respect, give you the confidence to stick up for your rights and protect them, and remain true to yourself, your wants and your needs. While self-confidence is an important aspect of assertiveness, it's crucial that you make sure that it doesn't develop into a sense of self-importance. Your rights, thoughts, feelings, needs, and desires are just as important as everyone else's, but not more important than anyone else's.

2. Voice Your Needs and Wants Confidently

If you're going to perform to your full potential then you need to make sure that your priorities – your needs and wants – are met. Don't wait for someone else to recognize what you need. You might wait forever! Take the initiative and start to identify the things that you want now. Then, set goals so that you can achieve them.

Once you've done this, you can tell your boss or your colleague exactly what it is that you need from them to help you to achieve these goals in a clear and confident way. And don't forget to stick to your guns. Even if what you want isn't possible right now, ask whether you can revisit your request in six months' time.

Find ways to make requests that avoid sacrificing others' needs. Remember, you want people to help you, and asking for things in an overly aggressive or pushy way is likely to put them off doing this and may even damage your relationship.

3. Acknowledge That You Can't Control Other People's Behaviour

Don't make the mistake of accepting responsibility for how people react to your assertiveness. If they, for example, act angry or resentful toward you, try to avoid reacting to them in the same way.

Remember that you can only control yourself and your own behavior, so do your best to stay calm and measured if things get tense. As long as you are being respectful and not violating someone else's needs, then you have the right to say or do what you want.

4. Express Yourself in a Positive Way

It's important to say what's on your mind, even when you have a difficult or negative issue to deal with. But you must do it constructively and sensitively. Don't be afraid to stand up for yourself and to confront people who challenge you and/or your rights. You can even allow yourself to be angry! But remember to control your emotions and to stay respectful at all times.

5. Be Open to Criticism and Compliments

Accept both positive and negative feedback graciously, humbly and positively. If you don't agree with criticism that you receive then you need to be prepared to say so, but without getting defensive or angry. The Feedback Matrix is a great tool that can help you to see past your emotional reactions to feedback, and instead use it to achieve significant, positive change.

6. Learn to Say "No"

Saying "No" is hard to do, especially when you're not used to doing it, but it's vital if you want to become more assertive.

Knowing your own limits and how much work you are able to take on will help you to manage your tasks more effectively, and to pinpoint any areas of your job that make you feel as though you're being taken advantage of. Remember that you can't possibly do everything or please everyone, so it's important that you protect your time and your workload by saying "no" when necessary. When you do have to say "no," try to find a win-win solution that works for everyone.

7. Use Assertive Communication Techniques

There are a number of simple but effective communication techniques that you can use to become more assertive. These are:

Use "I" Statements: Use "I want", "I need" or "I feel" to convey basic assertions and get your point across firmly. For example, "I feel strongly that we need to bring in a third party to mediate this disagreement."

Empathy: Always try to recognize and understand how the other person views the situation. Then, after taking her point of view into consideration, express what you need from her. For example, "I understand that you're having trouble working with Arlene, but this project needs to be completed by Friday. Let's all sit down and come up with a plan together."

Escalation: If your first attempts at asserting yourself have been unsuccessful, then you may need to escalate the matter further. This means becoming firmer (though still polite and respectful) with the person who you are requesting help from, and may end in you telling him what you will do next if you still aren't satisfied. For example, "John, this is the third time this week I've had to speak to you about arriving late. If you're late once more this month, I will activate the disciplinary process."

However, remember that, regardless of the consequences that you communicate to the person in question, you may still not get what you want in the end. If this is the case, you may need to take further action by setting up a formal meeting to talk about the problem or escalating your concerns to Human Resources (HR) or your boss.

Ask for More Time: Sometimes, it's best not to say anything. You might be too emotional or you might not know what it is that you want yet. If this is the case, be honest and tell the person that you need a few minutes to compose your thoughts. For example, you might say "Dave, your request has caught me off guard. I'll get back to you within the half hour."

Change Your Verbs: Try using verbs that are more definite and emphatic when you communicate. This will help you to send a clear message and avoid "sugar-coating" your message so much that people are left confused by what it is that you want from them. To do this, use verbs like "will" instead of "could" or "should," "want" instead of "need," or "choose to" instead of "have to."

For example: "I will be going on vacation next week, so I will need someone to cover my workload."

"I want to go on this training course because I believe that it will help me to progress in my role and my career."

"I choose this option because I think it will prove to be more successful than the other options on the table."

Be a Broken Record: Prepare the message that you want to convey ahead of time. If, for instance, you can't take on any more work, be direct and say, "I cannot take on any more projects right now." If people still don't get the message, then keep restating your message using the same language, and don't relent. Eventually, they will likely realize that you really mean what you're saying. For example:

"I'd like you to work on the Clancy project."

"I cannot take on any more projects right now."

"I'll pay extra for you to do it."

"I cannot take on any more projects right now."

"Seriously, this is really important. My boss insists that this gets done."

"I cannot take on any more projects right now."

"Will you do it as a personal favor?"

"I'm sorry, I value our relationship but I simply cannot take on any more projects right now."

Be careful with the broken record technique. If you use it to protect yourself from exploitation, that's good. But if you use it to bully someone into taking action that's against their interests, it can be manipulative and dishonest.

Scripting: It can often be hard to know how to put your feelings across clearly and confidently to someone when you need to assert yourself. The scripting technique can help here. It allows you to prepare what you want to say in advance, using a four-pronged approach that describes:

- **The event.** Tell the other person exactly how you see the situation or problem.
- **Your feelings.** Describe how you feel about the situation and express your emotions clearly.
- **Your needs**. Tell the other person exactly what you need from her so that she doesn't have to guess.
- **The consequences**. Describe the positive impact that your request will have for the other person or the company if your needs are met successfully.

CHAPTER 5

SOCIAL INTELLIGENCE FOR BUSINESS

Social intelligence can be defined as the human ability of decoding the happenings of the world and responding to it likewise. This ability is exclusive to humans and distinguishes us from the rest of beings in the animal kingdom.

Social Intelligence is also the capability to act wisely while maintaining human relations. It is markedly different from just intelligence, unlike what people used to think earlier. Over the years, it has been observed that many exceptionally intelligent people struggle a lot while maintaining a social life.

An immediate example that springs to the mind is that of Kim Peek, whose life had inspired the hit movie, Rain Man. Peek had an exceptionally sharp memory that allowed him to literally scan through books reading two pages at a time, with his left eye reading the left page and the right eye going through the right page simultaneously. This technique allowed him to browse through books at incredible speeds and what he read, he remembered permanently. Last checked, he was about to recall paragraphs from over 12,000 books. However, he was socially inept and avoided human interaction for a major part of his life. His communication was, for the most part, limited to his father.

Examples such as these prove that even exceptionally intelligent people need not have the same levels of social intelligence too. Social Intelligence is different from academic ability and signifies the talent of getting along with other people, as compared to solving equations and having well-defined learning mental facilities. As per the recent definition, Social Intelligence is an individual's collection of knowledge and facts about the outside world. This can be influenced by factors like self-confidence, and a desire to meet new people.

Social Intelligence is also known as interpersonal intelligence because it is also the study of an individual's ability to notice the distinctions between him and other people. As per this concept, a person's own unique personality is a product of the person's difference in knowledge on different areas as well as the level of social interactions he has with the people in his surroundings.

Importance of Social Intelligence

Industry experts have confirmed that thousands of employees have recently lost their jobs due to their lack of social incompetence. Earlier, talented people thought they only have to be good at their jobs to guarantee their place in a company. However, the recent change in business approach has made all these employees rethink their style of working. They now realize that they can't be employees in desk-jobs, and have to start taking a larger interest and part in the improvement and growth of the organization.

Technology has made people self-centered, in the sense that people might be interacting with people online happily, but the same people will be ignoring those sitting beside them. This boundary that people have drawn around them makes them look isolated and uninterested in any real-world communication, making the lack of human communication and relationships a pressing problem of our times.

It is no surprise then that people having better social skills have more friends, are in more relationships, and know how to nurture a relationship. This leads them to have successful careers and generally happier lives.

We live in a society and come in contact with people with different thoughts and personalities every day. While meeting these people with different social and psychological characteristics, we experience happiness, sorrow, misunderstandings, agreements, quarrels, and other different emotions. If we don't know how to handle these feelings, we will tend to avoid those people who make us feel uncomfortable. That in turn, will make us appear unfriendly to those people, many of whom could be important people in our lives.

People with high social intelligence understand the emotions of other people and are also able to control their own emotional responses to these situations. They can know why people behave the way they do. They understand different points of view and know how to respond to conflicting situations with calmness and composure. These qualities make a person an ideal employee and this why people who compete for jobs realize that social intelligence cannot be taken for granted. It brings balance and a sense of perspective in one's life and thus, is very essential to the growth of individuals.

What would be the benefit of improving the social intelligence of employees in an organization? Sample this. After integrating a six-month training process called "Emotional Intelligence for New Managers" to their training program, FedEx reported an 8-11% increase in core leadership competencies. Over half the participants have shown very large (10-50%) improvements in their emotional intelligence skills, like leadership abilities. 72% of the program participants are exhibiting tremendous improvement in their decision-making skills, over 60% report a better quality of life and 58% show much-improved decision-making skills.

Socially Intelligent People

Daniel Goleman has stated in his book "Social Intelligence" that the worst side of human nature is the toxic form it can take by just being around the wrong person at the wrong time. This extremely popular book was influential in bringing a sea of change in the way companies viewed the roles of employees in the company.

Employees were earlier treated and looked as service-providers, however, now the employees are treated like an organization's key assets. These changes have come due to the companies' adopting the applications of

Social Intelligence in their day-to-day lives in workplace.

According to Social Intelligence experts, no two humans have an identical interpretation of the same word. The word 'car' might bring the mental image of a Barracuda for someone, while someone else could imagine an Aston Martin. Human beings respond to words through the inputs they get and their own sensibilities.

 In many situations, the messages are sent via postures, movements, gestures, facial expressions and tone of voice. For example, if you were to walk into a conference room where a meeting is on the way, you can easily be able to figure out who the influential people are and who are the subordinates by simply observing their way of sitting, the way people respond to them, the way someone stands or maintains eye contact, etc.

The manner in which a person can influence others through his physical appearance, mood, body language, even the space he occupies in the room has a bearing upon the others and are clues to the way the person desires to be talked to, listened to, and respected.

Many tend to believe that only good looks and good clothes are sufficient to send a suitable message across, however, the physicality of a person bears huge significance on the way he portrays emotions of friendliness, effectiveness, assurance, kindness, and empathy. They need to project an inviting personality that dispels the initial hiccups in the mind of a person while approaching them.

When people sense hostility or are themselves unwilling to accept a decision, they start sending subtle, sometimes obvious, signals through their body language. These signals are found to be in direct conflict to the put-on neutrality they try to portray in their speech. People are quick to observe if a person has a salesman smile, i.e. insincere smile where he is trying to be too friendly, as opposed to the normal behavior.

Putting it differently, you could say that the person will give off the air of not being authentic. Authenticity is different from being merely honest and true. An authentic person is someone who also portrays genuine emotions for people and wants to really help others. Just having a good smile and good personality is not sufficient if a person is not authentic. Therefore, a person who has good social skills might not be able to impress upon people if he is not socially intelligent.

Socially intelligent people also know the difference between people who are genuinely hurt, and those who are looking for an excuse to make you feel bad for hurting them. These people have low self-esteem and love playing the victim card. They believe that by complimenting others, they degrade themselves, hence they enjoy making people fall for their guilt trap. For example, if you confront these people on their poor performance, then these kind of people will often come up with a left-handed comment like, "how could you say that after all that I have been through in my life recently?", clearly trying to attach their issues in family life to their drop in productivity at the workplace.

A socially intelligent person knows that empathizing with them is just feeding to their negative self-esteem, hence he will steer clear of getting too involved in giving suggestions to them. On the contrary, he will stick to the point and send polite reminders about the work that needs to be done.

According to Eric Berne, people who have had neglected, abused, or generally bad childhoods have trouble in building relationships or having self-esteem. These people feel neglected even in their adult life and their sense of low self-esteem prevents them from having an honest, frank, and direct interaction with anyone.

What these people do is manipulate other people's emotions and make them do what they want when they could have achieved the same results just by asking politely. Identifying these people is the first step to building a good task force. People with high emotional intelligence, on the other hand, will always have a strong elevator speech to describe or introduce any idea to people.

They always know how to put important concepts, ideas, or situations in front of others in a concise, clear, and objective manner. This helps them in putting an honest impression in the minds of their listeners while bringing the focus on the task in hand. At a time when getting more messages across consistently is becoming the need of the hour, having the skill of making efficient and specific communication with others is a big advantage.

Another ability that people with good social intelligence have is to be able to use language that can express tough feedback and criticism in a more palatable manner. Nobody generally likes to face criticism, as they consider it to be a judgment on their efforts. So an employee needs to be properly conditioned to accept criticism in a positive manner, however giving criticism in a positive manner in itself is an art that requires great practice and right choice of words.

Socially intelligent people have the ability to know how to monitor their language in such a manner that it avoids any conflict in the minds of the listeners. They can identify words that might create misunderstanding and steer clear of these ambiguous words.

They also realize that certain words tend to intimidate and threaten people. They avoid the usage of such words, especially while sharing feedback on the people's performances. They do it through their skills of empathy and being open-minded towards people's queries. For example, instead of using "you" statements, they focus more on using "I" statements.

Sample the following conversations:

Case 1: Team Manager to employee: "You are always coming late and giving excuses. Your output has been very low this month and your performance is nothing to write home about. You have not delivered anything last month and now you face termination from the company."

Case 2: Team Manager to employee: "I am concerned about how I am going to put good numbers on the board this month, as I haven't yet received the productivity that I was expecting. I am also thinking seriously about the punctuality issue of our team and how that is making us lose productivity. The performance of our team last year was also not satisfactory and I am under pressure to trim off those from the team who are not pulling their weight."

Of both, the cases, which one do you think will get the message across and prevent any negative personal backlash? Which case would get the employee start thinking without feeling bad about his performance being pointed out to him?

A person with Social Intelligence knows that using the 'I' statements will show the employee the issues that the manager is facing and what he is forced to deal with, and also makes the person being spoken to sensitive to the issues. Using neutral language will send a positive signal of mutual respect to the listener and a willingness to acknowledge a different point of view.

As you can see, the changes that you are to bring in your speech are not vast. It's just the change of one word in the previous example that set off a completely different course of conversation and interpretation. For example, many language specialists say that using the word 'but' signifies a precondition to an action.

In the sentence, "I will help you, but you have to wait for just a few minutes." signifies a precondition that help will only be provided in case you are patient. However, substituting the 'but' with 'and' will make the sentence sound different. Try it yourself:

I will help you, and you have to wait for just a few minutes.

People who haven't acquired clarity in speech tend to speak in a cluttered, rambling manner which clearly suggests that they haven't yet learnt how to process and filter their thoughts. A carefully constructed conversational strategy requires the proper usage of words and also the proper intonation.

Influencing others needs information to be presented in such a manner that can be easily processed. It's also important to present the right picture. Before giving a statement, it's always advisable to ask yourself - Do you say what you mean and mean what you say?

CHAPTER 6

WORKPLACE AND INTERVIEWS

Effective communication in the workplace is key to establishing strong relationships and getting important projects done. Communication doesn't only feel good, it also shows results. According to a Watson Wyatt study, companies that communicate the most effectively are 50% more likely to report low turnover levels compared with the industry average. Of course, everyone struggles with communication from time to time, which can lead to misunderstandings and frustrations.

To help solve for these issues, I've come up with some easy tips you can start using today to improve the communication skills and overall relationships between you and your teammates.

Establish A Foundation First. The more an employee trusts you, the more likely they are to come forward and communicate when a problem is occurring. A great way to lay that foundation is to establish a rapport with your employee first. The more an employee trusts you, the more likely they are to come forward and communicate when a problem is occurring.

Prove Through Your Words And Actions That You're Trustworthy. According to the American Psychological Association, nearly one-quarter of employees don't trust their employer. It sounds simplistic, but it's true: proving trustworthy to your employees will result in effective business communication time and again. The core of this issue is straightforward: Show a genuine interest in the person, empathize with their roadblocks or dilemmas, and follow through on the ways you say you will help. Your employee will be much more likely to communicate a challenge when they know they can trust you to stay level headed and work together to find a solution.

Set Up Weekly Or Monthly 1:1s. Sometimes, all it takes to open up lines of communication is setting a time to do so. Your employee might worry that she's burdening you during the day if you're busy and she wants to share recent challenges, concerns, or even triumphs. By setting up a recurring meeting to touch base, you'll learn more about the inner workings of what's going on the office and have a better idea on how to iron out the kinks.

Explain Why You're Asking Your Employee To Do Something. This one might sound silly to you. Doesn't Alfred know why creating that slide deck to present to the sales team is important? Without sounding condescending, there is a definite way to share the importance of a task you assigned and frame it in a positive and informative way. For example, along with this assignment, you could tell your employee, "These slides are a great way to communicate with the sales team how marketing is supporting their efforts. Do you have any questions on the approach or how you want to present it?" By doing so, you're offering vital information and the opportunity to ask questions they may have hesitated to communicate otherwise. Perhaps more importantly, you're also showing the employee how their work ties directly to business goals.

Really Listen. People often think of communication as getting your own message across, but effective communication really is a two-way street. If you're not actively listening to what the other person is saying, it's difficult to end up on the same page. Ask questions for clarification, and give the conversation your full attention. Avoid multitasking, or thinking of your response before the other person is done talking. Active listening can be challenging, but it's worthwhile.

Avoid Making Quick Assumptions. One of the biggest inhibitors to quality communication in the workplace is missed signals and quickly formed assumptions. If your employee is lagging in an area in which you expected them to excel, don't immediately assume that they're a slacker who doesn't care. Instead, provide a non-confrontational setting to dig into where the problems lie. When you ask your employee how things are going, you may find out that they are moving and have had a hard time focusing at work, or that they're not used to juggling six projects at once and need to de-prioritize something. When your ears are open, so are the lines of communication.

Learn Each Other's Strengths And Weaknesses. There's more than one way to do this. It might be through observation throughout the months, finding out what your team members are strong at and need a little help with. For example, my boss and I have figured out that she's great at getting work done in ordered and segmented blocks, whereas I get my best work done in concentrated bursts. There's also the personality type route - Enneagram, Myers Briggs, and Strengths Finder are just a few. All of a sudden, it might make sense that you're motivated by competition and focus, whereas your other teammate does best with input and ideation. By understanding each other's strengths and weaknesses, it's easier to have effective communication in the workplace.

Feel Out The Other Person's Preferred Communication Style. Maybe some of your team members are rarely on Slack, whereas others respond to emails instantly. How do your employees and teammates communicate on projects best? Do they prefer email, in-person chats, or Slack? You can learn this by asking them directly and also through observation.

Stay Consistent With Expectations And Follow Up. It's easy to drop regular check-ins when work gets busy, but it's one of the best ways to maintain effective workplace communication. Does your employee know when you're going to follow up about a project, and what elements you expect to see in their work? One of the most frustrating experiences as an employee is finishing a project and finding out your manager wanted something completely different. Prevent that by being clear and open to questions from the beginning.

Set The Tone For Meetings. What is the purpose of your meeting? Who will be running it? What is the agenda? Send out a meeting agenda via email before the meeting starts, so that everyone attending knows what to expect.

Offer Constructive Feedback In A Thoughtful Way. We've all been there before - aggressive and tone-deaf feedback from a manager that permanently wipes out trust and lines of communication. A starter tip? Focus on the behavior you're discussing, not the person's character. And always, always give the other person an opportunity to share their thoughts and contribute to building a positive process moving forward.

Offer Compliments In A Thoughtful Way. If you tell an employee they did a great job, the compliment isn't as helpful as you think. They may be left thinking, "But what was great about it? How can I replicate it if I don't know?" Be specific instead - "You did a great job explaining how leads convert into customers in that presentation. The visuals really helped the audience understand the process."

Keep Workflows Transparent. Say your team is working on a big project together. Does the team know the project's deadline, who is responsible for what parts of the project, and when they're expected to hand those parts off to other teammates? Organize a clear walkthrough by using Excel Spreadsheets or Trello, so all your team members are on the same page and not frustrated by miscommunications.

Make People's Role In A Group Or Project Clear From The Start. Communication in the workplace can break down fast when people don't understand their roles. This goes hand in hand with keeping workflows transparent. Establish the key stakeholders in the project, who has final approval, and what channels the project needs to go through for completion.

Decide Which Conversations Are Best For Which Venues. Beyond the normal level of social appropriateness - (no, you shouldn't ask about someone's family emergency in front of the whole team) - discuss with your team which modes of communication work best for which situations.

Use Modern Tools To Enhance - Not Truncate - Your Communication. Chat and email are great, to a point. However, if going back and forth on the computer is getting too complicated, don't be afraid to take the conversation off Slack and bring it face-to-face instead. It will probably simplify the task at hand and prevent miscommunications - like perceived sarcasm or reluctance.

Seek Out Feedback Regularly And Take It In Stride. Actively seeking out constructive feedback is one of the best ways to improve communication in the workplace. For example, after every 1:1 I have with my boss, we ask each other if there is any additional feedback to give. Some of it is positive - "I enjoyed seeing your work ethic this week when confronted with several different blockers," — and some of it is more constructive - "I noticed you expressed frustration during our brainstorming meeting this week." However, those moments of feedback are always an opportunity to get to the heart of a challenge or victory.

Make Processes Clear And Streamline Annoying Roadblocks. If you're working on a massive project with multiple stakeholders, chances are at some point or another there will be a lapse in communication. Take that lapse as an opportunity to improve upon the process the next time around. When you communicate these changes, you can also get helpful feedback on what is working for people and what isn't for the future.

Keep Related Parties In The Loop. Did part of a project get cut, or will a finished product require review from multiple parties in the company? Don't spring this information on your team members. Keep them in the loop and let them know ahead of time if something is coming around the bend. Everyone appreciates a heads up, and it will also be the perfect opportunity to communicate any other blockers that could arise before they become a last-minute problem.

Effective communication in the workplace means a foundation for success, both for your company and overall employee happiness.

How to Communicate Effectively in a Job Interview

Your communication skills play a significant role while you are interviewed for a job post. In fact, the way you communicate goes a long way in boosting your credentials mentioned on your resume. Based on recent job profiles it can be safely said that commercial enterprises across the globe irrespective of their sizes have unanimously zeroed in on one quality for their potential employees and that is "good communication skills". It is very clear that you have to justify all your important degrees with good communicative attributes while interviewing for a job. Globalization is the chief reason why so much importance is attached to communication. The different IT, ITES companies, Union Public Service Commissions, State Public Service Commission, etc. are looking to hire smart and outgoing individuals with great communication skills besides other qualities.

Why does communication play a big role during interviews?

a) The modern age of globalization has sparked a number of tie-ups between companies of different nations. This necessitates the presence of extraordinary communication skills among workers.

b) Communication is also important when it comes to group dynamics. Lucid and timely communication of job responsibilities among a team ensures better execution.

c) Communication is the key factor in establishing relations among colleagues and different groups.

d) Good communication saves time and energy- an absolute need for industries working under strict deadlines.

e) Effective communication ensures better job performance.

f) You can turn an otherwise boring work environment into something very interesting by simply motivating your co-workers with your effective communication skills.

g) Pleasant and balanced communication skills might help you to leave a very favorable impression on the interviewer.

Before we start talking about how to maximize your communication skills during interviews, I'm going to share my single favorite tip for succeeding in job interviews. Just keeping this one simple fact in mind has helped me out in several job interviews so far, and helped a lot of my friends as well. After I share my tip, we'll talk about how important it is to demonstrate good communication skills during an interview, and why that's a lot easier than you might think, even if you're shy.

It sounds really simple because it is. Just remember this one thing: The reason you're in that interview room is because they want to hire you. It is the interviewer's job to find an appropriate candidate to fill the position, and they want it to be you because that makes their job easier. Whenever I go into an interview with this mind state, I'm filled with confidence because I feel like I already belong there. Communication skills are also crucial. Whether you're introverted or extroverted, both traits have their pros and cons but if you stick to the basics you'll do great.

Tips for Better Communication In Job Interviews

Ask Questions. Remember, you're there to be interviewed for the job but it works both ways - you need to ask some questions as well, in order to make sure the job is a good fit you for. It's a good idea to have at least a couple questions ready to ask, and a few more in mind in case the ones you were going to ask get answered before you have a chance. More than likely, the person conducting the interview will ask if you have any questions, and it shows that you've been putting thought into this and that you came prepared.

Speak Clearly And Thoughtfully. Adjust your volume for the environment and make sure the interviewer can hear and understand you easily. Don't rush yourself and take time to deliver thoughtful responses. Ask for clarification if you don't understand a question.

Be Conscious Of Your Posture. You will want to sit up straight (no leaning or lounging) and avoid crossing your arms in front of your chest (it can seem defensive or withdrawn).

Make Eye Contact. Look at the interviewer while they ask you questions and give them non-verbal cues - smiling, nodding - when appropriate. Make it clear that you understand what they're saying, that you're listening.

Project Calm. Fidgeting and extra movement can make you seem nervous even if you aren't. Be aware of your tendencies and try to minimize them. If you know you fidget, try to keep your hands folded and avoid clicking or tapping the pen. Don't wear jewelry that you will play with or that will make noise while you move. Wear your hair in a way that will not tempt you to touch or play with it constantly. If seated at a table, sit towards the front of the chair and plant your feet on the floor - it can help keep you steady.

Negotiating Your Way To A Better Situation. This will apply more to positions requiring specialized skills rather than entry-level jobs where you typically won't have as much leverage. Once a job offer has been made, you can certainly accept it as-is but this may be a good time to try to negotiate better terms for yourself, whether it's to be reviewed for a raise sooner, or a better parking spot, or what have you. It's important to examine who has more power in this position, and it can be a risky move to ask for too much - especially if you getting the offer instead of something else came down to a coin-toss. Negotiating for value can be very rewarding, but make sure you know what you're doing!

Listen And Focus. When someone is explaining a lot of things in a job interview, it can be easy to lose focus and to start to daydream, especially when nerves are involved. It's important to be aware of this going in, and to do your best to pay close attention. Nothing looks works than asking a question that's just been explained to you while you were daydreaming.

Be The Best Representation Of Yourself. It's important to be yourself in a job interview, but don't act like the person conducting the interview is one of your college buddies. Stay professional, even if the interview is casual and relaxed. There's no point in putting on a complete facade for an interview because at the end of the day if you get the job, you want to be comfortable at work. You can communicate professionalism, by the way, your carry yourself from the moment you enter the building, to the way you dress and even making sure your shoes are clean. A lot of communication happens without saying a word.

CHAPTER 7

EFFECTIVE STRATEGIES AND TECHNIQUES

Communication is becoming more and more difficult to master because so few people actually utilize the three forms. While people are constantly connected, they are also detached by their heavy reliance on smartphones and other mobile devices.

Here we've collected the top communication techniques and strategies designed to help you learn to communicate properly.

Strategies For Active Listening

The following strategies are intended to promote active listening or a type of listening with the goal to develop a clear understanding of the speaker's concern and also to clearly communicate the listener's interest in the speaker's message.

Stop. Focus on the other person, their thoughts and feelings. Consciously focus on quieting your own internal commentary, and step away from your own concerns to think about those of the speaker. Give your full attention to the speaker.

Look. Pay attention to non-verbal messages, without letting yourself be distracted. Notice body language and non-verbal cues to allow for a richer understanding of the speaker's point. Remember that active listeners need to communicate to the speaker that they are involved and giving the person unconditional attention.

Listen. Listen for the essence of the speaker's thoughts: details, major ideas, and their meanings. Seek an overall understanding of what the speaker is trying to communicate, rather than reacting to the individual words or terms that they use to express themselves.

Be Empathetic. Imagine how you would feel in their circumstances. Be empathetic to the feelings of the speaker, while maintaining a calm center within yourself. You need not be drawn into all of their problems or issues, as long as you acknowledge what they are experiencing.

Ask Questions. Use questions to clarify your understanding, as well as to demonstrate interest in what is being said.

Paraphrase. If you don't have any specific questions to ask, you may choose to repeat back to the speaker, in your own words, what you have taken away, in order to allow the speaker to clarify any points.

Strategies For Accurate Perception

Analyze Your Own Perceptions. Question your perceptions, and think about how they are formed. Check in with others around you regularly, and be aware of assumptions that you are making. Seek additional information and observations. You may just need to ask people if your perceptions are accurate.

Work On Improving Your Perception. Increase your awareness of barriers to perception, and which ones you tend towards. Check in with yourself regularly. Seek honest, constructive feedback from others regarding their perceptions of you as a means of increasing your self-awareness.

Focus On Others. Develop your ability to focus on other people, and understand them better by trying to gather knowledge about them, listening to them actively, and imagining how you would feel in their situation.

Strategies For Effective Verbal Communication

Focus On The Issue, Not The Person. Try not to take everything personally, and similarly, express your own needs and opinions in terms of the job at hand. Solve problems rather than attempt to control others. For example, rather than ignoring a student who routinely answers questions in class with inappropriate tangents, speak with the student outside of class about how this might disrupt the class and distract other students.

Be Genuine Rather Than Manipulative. Be yourself, honestly and openly. Be honest with yourself, and focus on working well with the people around you, and acting with integrity.

Empathize Rather Than Remain Detached. Although professional relationships entail some boundaries when it comes to interaction with colleagues, it is important to demonstrate sensitivity and to really care about the people you work with. If you don't care about them, it will be difficult for them to care about you when it comes to working together.

Be Flexible Towards Others. Allow for other points of view, and be open to other ways of doing things. Diversity brings creativity and innovation. Value yourself and your own experiences. Be firm about your own rights and needs. Undervaluing yourself encourages others to undervalue you, too. Offer your ideas and expect to be treated well.

Use Affirming Responses. Respond to others in ways that acknowledge their experiences. Thank them for their input. Affirm their right to their feelings, even if you disagree. Ask questions, express positive feeling; and provide positive feedback when you can.

CHAPTER 8

LOVE AND COMMUNICATION

No matter how experienced you may be in the dating department, one thing remains constant: Effective communication in a relationship is crucial during every stage, whether it's making clear what you both want in the short- and long-term to defining clear boundaries in the bedroom and beyond. Even couples that appear to be effortlessly happy will admit that romance is only part of the equation to maintaining a loving and healthy relationship - and once you transition from the honeymoon phase into that let's get serious territory, it can be tricky to navigate your way through new situations, especially as you and your partner are still getting acquainted with each other's temperaments.

Before you work on improving the communication in your relationship, you need to realize that not everyone has the same communication preferences. Some people like to talk, some prefer touch and others are more visual or respond better to gift giving than an outward discussion of feelings. You probably know which communication style you prefer, but what about your partner's? We are all unique, and we all respond to different stimuli in distinct ways, and effective communication with your partner will come from acknowledging this. Your partner may be telling you exactly what they need, but you have to be cognizant of how they convey this information to you. If there's miscommunication, you'll miss the opportunity to build trust and intimacy, and you'll both feel frustrated within the relationship.

Watch your partner respond to different perceptive cues over a day or two. Does he or she seem to respond most to seeing and watching? Hearing and talking? Or touching and doing? For example, if your partner is more responsive to language, tone, and other auditory cues, making lots of eye contact and gentle facial expressions may not be communicating as much to them as you think. You're sending signals but they're not picking them up. On the other hand, if you find that you are an auditory person and your partner is a kinesthetic person, remember that saying "I love you" may not be enough: Reinforce your love with touch, and remember to do so often.

Use these tips on effective communication in a relationship to better the relationship, and understand your partner for who they really are as an individual, behind the facade of love.

Be Present In Your Relationship. To truly understand what your partner is telling you, be present, be here now: Put time aside and dedicate yourself 100% to communicating with your partner. They should know, truly feel, that they have your full attention and that they are your number one priority. It's difficult to listen and be fully present, aware and mindful when you're angry and stressed or are working on things that take time away from your relationship, but remember that intimacy, love, and trust are built when times are hard, not when they're easy. If we gave up at every sign of resistance, we would never progress and evolve. Seize these opportunities to grow and flourish with your partner.

Understand Each Other As You Change. Our likes and dislikes change all the time. Talk to your partner about each other's interests and dreams, what either of you want to be doing a few years down the lane, and where both of you should go on a vacation the next time around. Ask about your partner's day at work, and find out about their friends and all the other little details. When you show interest in each other's lives, you understand each other better and improve communication in a relationship.

Learn To Be Frank In Love. Communication in a relationship isn't just about talking with each other or having a laugh. It's also about expressing a negative opinion once in a while even if it sounds harsh. Withholding your frustration won't stop your partner from doing the same thing again. If something hurts you or is holding your partner back from achieving something better, talk about it when the time's right.

One of the biggest mistakes couples do is expect their partner to read their mind. Yes, you've been together for a long time, but that's no reason to become mind readers. Even the best of lovers can overlook a few details now and then. So if something's bothering you, learn to speak out the very instant it bothers you.

Go Out One Day In A Week. You and your lover may be spending your evenings together, but are you really spending time with each other? Most of us watch the television while having dinner, and even while lying in bed. When you're just spending time together without really talking, there's no communication in the relationship. To increase communication in a relationship, make plans with your partner to go out at least one evening in a week. It doesn't always have to be dinner, even spending a couple of hours in a café can make for a lot of great conversations that can be fun and bring both of you closer.

Do Things Together During The Weekends. Do either of you like gardening, or rock sculpting, or perhaps even cooking exotic dishes? It doesn't matter what both of you like, as long as something interests you. Weekend afternoons are a great time to do something together. A beautiful weekend afternoon is warm and lazy, and spending time together during this part of the day can feel refreshing to both of you, and the relationship.

Lies And Sugarcoated Confessions. To build effective communication in a relationship, you need to learn to be truthful. By lying or feeling suspicious about your partner, you're not helping the communication in the relationship. Be truthful with each other and never give your partner the opportunity to doubt you. Think your co-worker is the sexiest thing you've ever seen? Fantasized about someone else last night? Your partner's been putting on a lot of weight recently? Is the sex getting really monotonous? Tell the truth to your partner but of course, don't talk about such details straight out. At times like these, make sure you bring the conversation up, but don't be so direct about it. Always make sure you speak your mind, but it's alright to sugarcoat your truth and mention it in passing, so it doesn't hurt your partner. But always speak out about everything on your mind, it's the only way to build trust and improve effective communication in a relationship.

Talk About Your Sexual Fantasies. This is one of the biggest things that matter in building effective communication in a relationship. Many partners want to do so many things in bed, but they just don't know how to say it out in fear of being judged or rebuked. Some partners like tantric sex or talking dirty, some want to role play in bed, a few have sexual fetishes, and others want to start swinging or indulge in exhibitionism and public flashing. You know what, all these things are completely acceptable as long as it's fun for both partners. Humans are creative creatures, so if you've got an active sexual imagination, why is that a bad thing? Sexual communication in a relationship is crucial for any relationship to succeed. If both of you aren't open sexually, it may lead to boring sex lives and one of you may even decide to have an affair with someone else. Learn to speak your mind in bed, even if it feels awkward. You don't need to talk about it straight out, drop a few hints and see how your partner responds. And if your partner's hinting something unconventional in bed, don't brush it away. Give it a thought if it's what your partner likes and wants.

Acknowledge Your Partner's Thoughts. Learn to understand your partner and at times, talk to your partner like you would with a best friend. If you find your partner glancing very discreetly at a girl who looks quite good, don't give him a bad stare and get huffy. Instead, acknowledge it and laugh about it. Instead of telling him to stop staring at her, tell him "she's quite pretty, isn't she?" By acknowledging it, you're letting your partner know that these passing glances are natural. Your partner may feel embarrassed, but they would understand the faith you have in them.

When Communication Goes Awry: How To Break The Pattern

You know what your partner needs, and have thought about their preferred communication style, but there's something else that affects communication in relationships: How you're speaking. Experts on communication and voices break down the way we talk into pitch, pace, volume, and timbre. The next time you're in a disagreement with your partner, be mindful and make conscious efforts to modulate these aspects of your voice.

A voice that is overly high-pitched sounds defensive and immature. Also, if you end a sentence with a higher pitch, it sounds like a question; don't do this unless you're actually asking a question, or you may instill doubt in your partner.

Pace just means how fast you're talking. Take a deep breath and slow down - especially when you're disagreeing. Speak calmly and clearly to get your message across. Pay attention to volume, especially volume "creep," and avoid competing to be heard - competition only leads to shouting and miscommunication. Being louder won't help you communicate with your partner. In fact, if your partner is speaking, you should listen.

Timbre refers to your voice's emotional quality, attitude, and tone. Pay careful attention to this, and watch for red flag timbres like sarcasm that can lead to a lack of communication and cause distrust in relationships.

When things do get out of hand, break the pattern: Be playful and use humor in a way that keeps the conversation flowing in the right direction. Injecting humor into the situation can make it feel less dire and can yield amazing results for the two of you. That's because humor helps you regain perspective and balance; it is an essential component of healthy communication in relationships. It also relieves stress and improves your physical happiness in your everyday life. The biggest benefit to laughing in this context is that it reminds you that you love just being together with your partner. It reminds you that you can enjoy your time together, even when things seem challenging.

It's important to break the pattern of hostility, hurt and retreat. For example, when you catch yourself raising your voice or being sarcastic, change your tone. If you're using "you" repeatedly and blaming your partner, switch to "I" and "me," or better yet, "we." There's no point in offloading all your relationship's issues on to your partner. There are two people in every relationship, so don't shift the blame to be entirely on their shoulders.

CHAPTER 9

NON-VERBAL COMMUNICATIONS

Non-verbal communication plays an important role in our daily life. More than90% of all the communication we use in our daily life to share information is supported by body language. Non-verbal communication can be defined as the process of sending and receiving messages via means other than words, like facial expressions, gestures, behavior, tone of voice, etc.

This is why we should pay extra special attention to this topic and try to learn more about our gestures, expressions, and behavior. Once we are able to understand our body language and other aspects of non-verbal communication, we will be able to communicate more easily with other people and we will find it easier to avoid misunderstandings.

In order to understand body language and other aspects of non-verbal communication, we need to focus on our behavior during the conversation. Our body sends out signals no matter where we are, what we are doing or the time of the day. Our body does not know how to lie; it cannot "be turned off". Our opinion is based on both the words we hear and the signals we receive from the other person via their body language. This is why we are able to like somebody, even though we have never spoken with that person. In this case, our opinion is based on the signals we receive from that person.

This chapter will talk about certain aspects of non-verbal communication. We will focus on gestures, facial expressions, eye contact, hand gestures, body postures, the way we move, tone of voice and the way we wear our clothes.

The importance of non-verbal communication increases when we are faced with a different culture, especially in the case when we do not speak the language very well and we need to use our hands in order to support our vocabulary. We have to be careful about our body language and gestures as every culture uses non-verbal communication in a different way. Some cultures express themselves by using a lot of body language (e.g. southern Europe), whereas it is almost hidden by other cultures (e.g. Japan). From my personal experience, I saw that Japanese body language is hidden and the gestures are done very subtly, nevertheless, non-verbal communication plays a big role in how people communicate with each other. Even if gestures are not very explicit, we should not underestimate the power of non-verbal communication. These subtle gestures can have an even stronger meaning than one may expect in comparison to their own culture. Therefore we should focus on these gestures, being very aware of them and try to decode even the smallest detail in the body language of a person.

Types of Nonverbal Communication

Eye Contact. Eye contact, an important channel of interpersonal communication, helps regulate the flow of communication. And it signals interest in others. Furthermore, eye contact with audiences increases the speaker's credibility. Teachers who make eye contact open the flow of communication and convey interest, concern, warmth, and credibility.

Facial Expressions. A look on a person's face can show their thoughts and feelings, communicating their emotions through a smile, frown, raised eyebrow, yawn or sneer. The area around the eyes and mouth transmits a large volume of information. Facial expressions continuously change during interaction and are constantly observed by the recipient. Therefore, the receiver's own emotional state is a crucial factor in determining how the facial expressions are interpreted.

Facial expressions also relate to the facial features. A person's face is seen as an important source of information about their personality. For example, a person with a curved mouth is likely to be judged as friendly, cheerful, easy-going, kind, likable and with a sense of humor, intelligent, well-adjusted and so on.

Facial expressions (or all non-verbal communication) are used to display, conceal, and to fake emotions. We both consciously and subconsciously make facial expressions at any time throughout the day. We send and receive all kinds of messages to each other using facial expressions. Sometimes we pretend to be interested in something when really we are not or because we have already been told before. This behavior is sometimes essential to establish a good relationship with others.

If there is a conflict between the verbal and non-verbal message, the receiver tends to believe the non-verbal message because it is beyond the communicator's control and therefore more "truthful" and will better reflect the communicator's emotional state. This means that the receiver can rely heavily on the facial expressions of the sender to understand the meaning behind the words.

Gestures. If you fail to gesture while speaking, you may be perceived as boring, stiff and un-animated. A lively and animated style captures attention, makes the material more interesting, facilitates learning and provides a bit of entertainment. Head nods, a form of gestures, communicate positive reinforcement to students and indicate that you are listening.

Gestures are movements of the arms, legs, hands, and head. Some authors opine that gesture is the deliberate body movement as because they express specific and intentional meaning. For example; a wave of the hand has a specific meaning-"hello" or "good-bye"; a forefinger and a thumb touching to form a circle have the meaning -"ok".

Alike facial expressions, interpretations of some gestures also differ across cultures. For example, in Europe, raising thumb is used to convey that someone has done something excellent while in Bangladesh the same gesture means something idiotic.

Posture And Body Orientation. You communicate numerous messages by the way you walk, talk, stand and sit. Standing erect, but not rigid, and leaning slightly forward communicates to receivers that you are approachable, receptive and friendly. Furthermore, interpersonal closeness results when you and your receiver face each other. Speaking with your back turned or looking at the floor or ceiling should be avoided; it communicates disinterest to your class.

Body Language. Body language is another widely recognized form of non-verbal communication. Body movements can convey meanings and message. Body language may take two forms of unconscious movements and consciously controlled movements.

For example; when a person is bored, he may gaze around the room rather than look at the speaker or he may shift positions frequently. When a person is nervous, he may bite his nails or mash hair. These are usually made unconsciously. On the other hand, leaning forward toward the speaker to express interest is the case of conscious body movements.

Space and Distance. Space and distance are significant non-verbal tools in the case of organizational communication. A spacious and well-decorated room indicates a person's position in the organization hierarchy and external people gets a message about his importance and authority only by visiting his room. Distance is another communication tool, which expresses the degree of intimacy and individual acceptance.

Proximity. Cultural norms dictate a comfortable distance for interaction with students. You should look for signals of discomfort caused by invading students' space. Some of these are:

- Rocking
- Leg swinging
- Tapping
- Gaze aversion

Typically, in large college classes space invasion is not a problem. In fact, there is usually too much distance. To counteract this, move around the classroom to increase interaction with your students. Increasing proximity enables you to make better eye contact and increases the opportunities for students to speak.

Para-linguistic. This facet of nonverbal communication includes such vocal elements as:

- Tone
- Pitch
- Rhythm
- Timbre
- Loudness
- Inflection

For maximum teaching effectiveness, learn to vary these six elements of your voice. One of the major criticisms is of instructors who speak in a monotone. Listeners perceive these instructors as boring and dull. Students report that they learn less and lose interest more quickly when listening to teachers who have not learned to modulate their voices.

Humour. Humour is often overlooked as a teaching tool, and it is too often not encouraged in college classrooms. Laughter releases stress and tension for both instructor and student. You should develop the ability to laugh at yourself and encourage students to do the same. It fosters a friendly environment that facilitates learning. Obviously, adequate knowledge of the subject matter is crucial to your success; however, it's not the only crucial element. Creating a climate that facilitates learning and retention demands good nonverbal and verbal skills.

Touch. Touch is a widely used form of non-verbal communication tool. By touching, one can express a wide range of emotions. However, the accepted modes of touch vary depending on the gender, age, relative status, intimacy and cultural background of the persons. For example, in the context of our culture, when one touches you from the back of the examination hall, your understanding is that he wants to know something.

Silence. Silence is a powerful tool for communication. It may have a positive or negative meaning. In a classroom, silence indicates that students are listening carefully and attentively. In the same way, through silence one can communicate his lack of interest or a failure to understand. For example, silence often indicates that a person receiving instruction does not understand the action required or sometimes silence indicates consent.

Personal Appearance. Appearance is also an important non-verbal communication tool. Appearance includes dress, hair, jewelry, makeup, belt buckles and so on. Appearance indicates the degree of importance or interest a person conveys to an occasion. By means of uniform, we can identify a student, a doctor, a lawyer, a police officer, etc. In an organization, one's dress is keenly observed to see whether it conforms to accepted standards of appearance. As an example, workers may wear different clothes when they are on strike than they do when they are working.

Symbol. A symbol is something which represents an idea, a physical entity or a process but is distinct from it. The purpose of a symbol is to communicate meaning. For example, a red octagon may be a symbol for "stop". On a map, a picture of a tent might represent a campsite.

Numerals are symbols for numbers. Personal names are symbols representing individuals. A red rose symbolizes love and compassion.

Visual Communication. When communication occurs by means of any visual aids, it is known as visual communication. Thus, communication that occurs through facial expression, personal appearance, gesture, posture, printed picture, sign, signal, symbol, map, poster, slide, chart, diagram, graph, etc. is called visual communication. For example, to indicate 'danger', we use red sign; to mean 'dangerous', we use a skull placed between two pieces of bone put in crosswise fashion; to indicate 'no smoking', we use an image showing a lighted cigarette with a cross mark on it.

Importance of Nonverbal Communication

Some important points expressing the importance, necessity, advantages or functions of non-verbal communication are discussed below:

Well Expression of the Speaker's Attitude. Various non-verbal cues of the speaker like physical movements, facial expression, a way of expression, etc. play important role in expressing the inner meaning of the messages in face-to-face conversation and interview. For example, the facial expression of the speaker indicates his attitude, determination depth of knowledge, etc.

Providing Information Regarding the Sender of The Written Message. The format, neatness, language and the appearance of the envelope used in a written message send a non-verbal message regarding the writer's tests, choice, level of education, etc.

Expressing the Attitude of the Listener and Receiver. Sometimes the appearance of the listeners and receivers conveys their attitudes, feelings, and thoughts regarding the messages they have read or heard.

Gaining Knowledge about a Class of People. Clothing, hairstyle, neatness, jewelry, cosmetics, and stature of people convey impressions regarding their occupation, age, nationality, social or economic level, job status, etc. For example; students, policemen, nurses, etc. can easily be identified through their dresses.

Gaining Knowledge about the Status of a Person. Non-verbal cues also help to determine the relative status of persons working in an organization. For example, room size, location, furnishings, decorations, lightings, etc. indicate the position of a person in the organization.

Communicating Common Message to All People. In some cases, non-verbal cues can effectively express many true messages more accurately than those of any other method of communication. For example; use of red, yellow and green lights and use of various signs in controlling vehicles on the roads.

Communicating with the Handicapped People. Non-verbal cues of communication greatly help in communicating with the handicapped people. For example; the language of communication with the deaf depends on the movements of the hands, fingers, and eyeball.

Conveying Message to the Illiterate People. Communication with illiterate people through written media is impossible. There may also be some situations that do not allow the use of oral media to communicate with them. In such situations, non-verbal methods like pictures, colors, graphs, signs, and symbols are used as the media of communication. For example; to indicate danger we use red sign and to mean dangerous we use a skull placed between two pieces of bone put in a crosswise fashion.

Quick Expression of Message. Non-verbal cues like sign and symbol can also communicate some messages very quickly than written or oral media. For example; when drivers of a running vehicle are to be communicated that the road ahead is narrow or there is a turn in the road ahead, we generally use signs or symbols rather than using any written or oral message.

Presenting Information Precisely. Sometimes quantitative information on any issue may require a lengthy written message. But this quantitative information can be presented easily and precisely through tables, graphs, charts, etc.

CHAPTER 10

BE AN AUTHORITY IN ANY SITUATION

I know how frustrating and painful it can be when you're not respected. People don't listen to you, they brush your feelings aside, they never pick your ideas. You just don't seem to matter to others. I also know that no matter where you're starting, you can quickly start getting more respected. All it takes is a few well-chosen steps in the right direction.

Here are the best steps to help you be an authority in different situations.

Make People Take You Seriously With This "Status Booster"

You shouldn't brag. But you also shouldn't be afraid to stand for what's good about you. Here are some examples of things we want to be able to stand by:

- "I work hard"
- "I'm a great friend"

- "I care a lot about other people"
- "I'm trustworthy and responsible"
- "I've overcome a lot of obstacles in my life"
- "I'm proud of who I am"

This doesn't mean you need to tell people these things directly. Instead, boost your social status through your actions:

- The jokes you make (a lot of self-deprecating humor, or humor that puts other people down, will not earn you respect)
- The things you laugh at (and, more importantly, refuse to laugh at)
- The places you go, things you do, and events you go to
- How you describe yourself, your work or your life when someone asks
- The things you post on social media (and the things you like/comment on)
- Keep in mind that humblebragging will not earn respect either.

What To Do When People Take You For Granted

If you feel like you're often taken advantage of or that you're too nice, then this is going to be extra important for you. The number one way to stop others from taking advantage of you is to set clear, enforceable boundaries. This method shows people they can't take you for granted and that you expect they treat you with respect.

When setting boundaries, first consider the things that you have control over. Don't set a boundary that you can't enforce. Let's say that you feel like your friend is taking advantage of you. They come over to your house any time they want, eat your food, and sleep on your couch. And they never ask for permission or contribute money for groceries. In this case, you can set a boundary that no one can come to your house between 9 pm and 9 am without your permission or invitation. Once you've decided what boundaries you need to set, you need to tell the person you're having a problem with.

There is almost always a reason why people do the things they do. It helps to consider the other person's situation. What could have made them act this way? Have they always taken you for granted?

You can even suggest ways that their needs can still be met without taking advantage of you. For example, ask your friends to call first if they need a place to sleep or contribute money if they frequently eat at your house. Even once you've set a boundary, there is a chance that they will cross the line. Sometimes people simply forget because they've been doing it like this for a long time. If this happens, your next step should be to have another conversation with them about it. Explain again:

- Why the things they're doing are problematic for you
- What your boundaries are
- And why you've set those boundaries

If they still don't respect your boundaries after that, you may need to make more drastic changes. Unfortunately, it might be necessary to cut contact with certain "friends".

How To Speak So People Listen To You

Many people who struggle with getting respect feel like they have no voice and nobody listens to them.

- Are people ignoring you, interrupting you, or talking over you?
- Are people not paying attention when you speak?
- Are your opinions overlooked or your feelings brushed aside?

Making yourself heard will help you develop more of a presence. That presence will earn you respect from the people close to you, both family, friends, and work colleagues.

- Use people's name when you're talking to them.
- Avoid overly complex language so that you are easily understood. People will resent you if they can't understand the words you use.

- Talk about things that interest the other person. A common mistake is to only talk about your own interests.
- Ask more questions about the other person – this will keep their focus on you.
- Use hand gestures to make your message stronger and clearer.
- Keep more eye contact. Make sure you give everyone in the group about equal eye contact to keep everyone's interest.
- Exercise your voice and articulation to get a strong voice that everyone hears.
- Minimize complaining and negativity. Make people feel good listening to you.
- Avoid bragging. People will see through it and think less of you for it.
- Use effectful pauses. Silence has a big impact on speech.
- Vary your tempo and tone when speaking. This makes you more interesting to listen to. Practice at home by recording yourself speaking.

- Ask people for feedback about how you can improve your speech.

Are You Apologizing For Your Mere Presence? Don't!

Imagine someone accidentally spilling their drink on you. Then, out of pure habit, you say "I'm sorry" even if you did nothing wrong and are now covered in beer. Over-apologizing is a sign that you're more submissive than dominant. While "submissive" and "dominant" can both be bad things in extremes, it's all about finding the right balance. You don't want to be a pushover or a doormat, but you don't want to be rude or arrogant either.

If you want to gain respect, you'll need to save your apologies for the times that you're actually sorry such as when you're the person that spills your beer on a stranger. Don't apologize for your mere presence, for stating your opinion, or for disagreeing. You don't need to apologize if you don't want to do something, either. Your opinions and presence matter, which means that you shouldn't apologize for just being around. Don't get stuck "sorry-ing" your way through life.

Use Your Body Language To Command Respect

Our body language can tell people how we feel about ourselves. If you walk around with your shoulders hunched, arms crossed, and eyes on the ground, you will seem shy, afraid, or insecure. None of that commands respect. However, if your body language portrays confidence, people will look up to you. They will believe that there must be a good reason for your confidence and therefore you must be worthy of their respect.

These are the characteristics of confident body language:

- Good eye contact when speaking and listening
- Good posture; no slouching or crossing your arms
- Walking with a purpose (not wandering around aimlessly)

- Keeping your chin up and eyes forward (instead of down)
- Use hand gestures when speaking (instead of keeping your hands shoved in your pockets)
- Keep in mind that while confident people earn respect, arrogant people lose it.

How To Stand Up For Your Opinions And Beliefs In A Respectful Way

When we compromise our beliefs to fit in, we disrespect ourselves. I have a friend who has traditional Christian beliefs. It's not very common where he lives in Sweden since most people are atheists over here. But everyone respects him.

Why? Because he doesn't push his beliefs onto anyone else and doesn't judge anyone for not sharing his belief. But when someone asks him about it, he always stands firm in his belief, while still being respectful and nice about it.

That's the sweet spot: Be comfortable both with your own beliefs and also with other differing beliefs. The most important thing you can do in any situation is make sure you are being heard. And I mean this literally.

If You Get Interrupted Or Cut Off, Make People Listen By Saying This

If your comment gets ignored or interrupted, you can say:

- "Just a second, I'd like to finish my thought."
- "Excuse me, we got off tracked. What I was saying was that _____."
- "Like I was saying before, _____."
- "Please, let me speak."

There are two more tactics I like when I want to say something but people keep talking over me:

Using people's motion-detecting to your advantage. You do this by raising your hand or your index finger briefly. This triggers people's motion detecting and makes them focus on you. This opens up a perfect

154

window for you to say something. If you don't get a window to say something immediately, that's okay. People will often remember that you got something to say, so they will give you a chance to speak later on in the conversation.

Using a quick inhale as a signal you got something to say. The same thing as the hand signal, by making a quick and audible inhale, people will notice you got something to say and focus on you. When you start asserting yourself more, people will become more aware of your presence and give you more space in conversations.

Note that all interruptions aren't made to belittle you. For example, in a lively group conversation, people interrupt each other all the time. That's okay and has nothing to do with being disrespectful. You'll just look like an asshole if you try to assert yourself every time. So, choose your fights wisely. And don't let others treat you like a doormat just because you're a nice person.

Are You Losing Your Temper And Getting Angry Too Easily?

I have a history of my emotions getting the better of me. I am working on it, but it has left such lasting damage that it feels like people are afraid of me. This makes me feel terrible now that I've grown up. I've realized the damage I made to my relationship by not having control over myself.

If you're prone to losing your temper or overreacting in certain situations, it's probably affecting the respect people have for you. If you lose your temper, people won't take you seriously because you seem so emotional and not logical. And some might even start avoiding you instead of talking with you.

Here's how to address a conflict in a way that makes people respect you more:

- Prepare some suggestions for improving the situation before you have a talk

- Have the conversation in private instead of making a scene in public
- Do it after you've cooled down instead of confronting someone in the heat of the moment
- Use "I feel" and, "I think" instead of making accusations such as "You always…"
- Keep yourself calm; make an effort not to get defensive or upset
- Be understanding of the other person's circumstances; tell them you understand and want to work with them to find a solution that works for both of you
- Be honest with yourself about mistakes you've made and things you could do differently moving forward
- Admit when you're wrong and apologize

Learning to keep your calm and to handle situations constructively will make people respect you. When you don't get mad every time, you will see how people start trusting you and talking more with you.

How You Can Improve Your Leadership Skills To Earn Respect At Work And In Life

Leadership makes people listen to you and it also helps you accomplish things at work and in life. Leadership is one of the most valued attributes from employers around the world. It will earn you respect at work. Being a leader means being a person who helps the group achieve their goals (goals can be both productive or just to have fun together).

Being a leader also means standing up for what you believe is right even if it goes against what others want or believe.

Here are some practical ways to earn respect by being a leader:

- Take initiative in situations where you are knowledgeable or skilled.
- Set short-term and long-term goals and come up with plans for achieving them.

- Make sure people hear you by speaking clearly and loudly.
- Keep your word - do what you say you're going to do.
- Lead by example - work hard if you want others to do the same.
- Do what you believe is right even if it's different than what everyone else is doing.
- Treat others with respect at all times.
- Don't lose your temper or blame others – focus on solving instead of blaming.

Self-Presentation: The Easiest Way To Double The Respect You Get?

The way you present yourself determines how people will see you and how much they will respect you.

Self-presentation includes:

- Dressing appropriately based on the situation
- Well-fitting and nice clothes
- Grooming (Showering, shaving, skin-care)

- Haircut
- Staying in shape

Things like clothes and looks might seem shallow, but people judge you a lot based on that. All those things represent both how you feel about yourself and how you want others to look at you. How you present yourself is especially important to make a great first impression. The cool thing about it is that most of these steps are super easy and effective ways to get more respect. All it takes is going to your hairdresser, taking a shower, shaving, or buying some new clothes.

It's just a few hours work each month and some of your hard-earned money to enjoy more respect for the rest of your life. Staying in shape is a bit more tricky and time-consuming, but there are also far more benefits to it.

How You Can Give Respect To Get Respect

Take a second to think about some of the most disrespectful people you've ever encountered. Do you respect those people? The answer is probably not.

The quickest way to shatter your reputation and lose respect is by speaking or behaving disrespectfully to someone else. Is it okay to get mad or upset or offended? Yes! You're human, and nobody can expect you to be perfect. But showing respect to people will go a long way towards earning respect from others even when they don't deserve it.

Here's why it works: When you behave respectfully you're proving that you're the bigger person. Your show of respect will show:

- Your self-control
- Your level-headedness
- Your ability to think on your feet
- Your ability to see beyond others weaknesses
- Your self-worth (you value yourself enough not to sink to others level)

All of those characteristics are worthy of respect. And you will earn that respect both from the person you responded to and from anyone who's watching. It says a lot when you refuse to treat someone poorly even when you could have.

You've probably heard the "Golden Rule": Treat others how you want to be treated. This is the basis of the concept of earning respect through giving it. You've probably had a bad day before, or a bad week, or even a bad year. Give other people the benefit of the doubt when they're behaving poorly. They may be going through something that you don't know about. Choose to treat them with respect anyway.

The Surprising Effect Of Owning Up To Your Mistakes

To see why it's so important to have the ability to admit when you're wrong, do this: Think about a person in your life who always refuses to admit when they've made a mistake. How do you feel about that person's behavior?

People who stand their ground even after they realize they've messed up are doing so out of pride. Prideful people quickly lose the respect of their peers. Be careful not to mistake "pride" with the idea of being proud of who you are. Being proud of who you are is a type of self-respect while being prideful is believing you're better than others.

Pride is an unattractive quality that ruins reputations and relationships. Admitting when you're wrong is always humbling. No one enjoys making mistakes. But the reality is that we all make mistakes, and each one of us is going to be wrong at some point.

Here are some things you can say when you realize you're in the wrong:

- "I've thought about what you said, and you're right."
- "I know I disagreed with you before, but what you said makes a lot of sense. You're right."
- "I'm sorry for what I said earlier. I was wrong about that."

Not only does admitting a mistake prevent you from looking foolish, it also shows the other person that you value them and their opinions. This will strengthen your relationship. But refusing to admit that you're wrong will push you away from each other. When I admit a mistake, I can almost feel how my relationship instantly improves. And I always learn something valuable from each time I'm wrong or mess up. When you're strong enough to admit your mistakes, you never have to be afraid to be wrong or mess up.

Be Taken More Seriously By Avoiding Self-Deprecating Humor

When you talk about yourself to others, what messages are you sending? Here are some examples of what type of messages self-deprecating humor can send:

- "I'm no good"
- "I'm terrible at everything"
- "I don't like myself"
- "You're better than me"
- "I'm not worth your time"

I realized that I talked down on myself by joking too much about myself. I communicated that I wasn't good enough. Self-deprecating humor can be great, but it should be obvious that there's no truth to it.

When Obama joked that he couldn't turn down the AC in the oval office, that was funny, because no one doubted his power. When I joke about being lonely on the weekends, it painted a picture of me as a lonely person, and it also communicated that I didn't respect myself.

Say This Instead Of "I'm Sorry" To Change How People Perceive You

A big problem with saying "I'm sorry" is that it gives the impression that you're in the wrong, even if you aren't. One way to stop saying "I'm sorry" too often is by replacing the phrase with a simple "Thank you" when it's possible. For example, if you're asking someone for something.

When you say "Thank you" instead of "I'm sorry," you're changing how the other person perceives you. "Thank you" shows appreciation to the other person for their time. It switches your mindset from an apologetic one to one of gratitude. The other person will also appreciate not needing to reassure you that you've done nothing wrong.

Another thing to say instead of "Sorry" is "Excuse me." If you bump into someone or need to get past them, saying "Excuse me" is a polite way to let them know without having to apologize for your presence.

Are You Losing Respect Because You Talk Too Much And Reveal Too Much About Yourself?

It's common to talk too much and start rambling when you get nervous or want to make a good impression. To gain others respect you can't just ramble and talk about yourself. You need to slow down and find some common ground first. That way people will start valuing your input and what you say.

Here are tips if you tend to talk too much or ramble about yourself:

- Think about what you want to say before you start speaking. That way your thoughts don't tumble out of your mouth in a complicated mess.
- Avoid using "uh" and "um" when you speak. Fillers like that that weaken your message and put you in a bad light.
- Start asking more questions and follow-up questions. This will slow down your pace and make sure you don't babble without any input from the other person.

- Avoid telling your whole life-story to others if they don't do the same.
- Share equally much about yourself as they share about themselves.
- Focus on finding mutual interests and talk about those. This makes sure the conversation is interesting for everyone involved.

Remember, it's all about taking one small step at a time. Take it at your own pace. Once you've mastered one respect tactic, choose another one to work on.

CHAPTER 11

EMPATHY AND COMMUNICATION

Empathy is the art of seeing the world as someone else sees it. When you have empathy, it means you can understand what a person is feeling in a given moment, and understand why other people's actions made sense to them. Empathy helps us to communicate our ideas in a way that makes sense to others, and it helps us understand others when they communicate with us. It is one of the foundational building blocks of great social interaction and, quite obviously, powerful stuff.

But how do you get empathy? How do you understand what someone else is feeling if that isn't happening automatically?

Well, to a certain extent we are all designed to naturally empathize with others. Our brains are wired to experience the emotions that someone else is feeling. That's why we wince when someone hits their hand with a hammer, or why we're more likely to laugh if someone else is laughing too. There's an excellent book called Social Intelligence on this topic which explains all of the research behind this natural empathy.

Unfortunately, only a few people have excellent natural empathy. Our empathic wiring exists on a continuum. Some people have fantastic natural empathy and can pick up how someone else is feeling just by looking at them. Some people have only a tiny amount of natural empathy, and won't notice that you are angry until you start yelling. Most people lie somewhere in the middle and understand how someone else is feeling only part of the time.

Fortunately, empathy is part talent and part training. Depending on your starting level of ability, getting better at empathy might require more or less work than someone else---but no matter what your starting point, you can teach yourself to be better at empathy. And this chapter is here to teach you how.

Empathy contains three lessons.

Understanding Yourself. If you want to understand the emotions of others, you have to learn to empathize with yourself. Understanding yourself was written to help you understand and accept your emotions. Understanding and accepting your own feelings is essential for a healthy life, and it's the foundation of empathizing with others.

Understanding Others. Through practice and a commitment to thoughtfulness, anyone can learn to understand how others are thinking and feeling. Understanding Others is the blueprint that shows you how.

Nonverbal Empathy. When you understand what someone else is thinking or feeling, it becomes easier to interact with them. But there's a nonverbal aspect to interaction that deserves special attention. The knowledge you gain from empathy can help you to use appropriate nonverbal communication. Nonverbal Empathy explains how.

So why exactly is empathy so important for us?

Humans Are Social Animals. No matter how you look at it, humans exist in communication with each other, and there are very few activities they take part in that don't include interactions with other human beings in this or that form. Therefore, it is hardly surprising that the ability to better understand others and read their feelings and emotions gives an edge to the one who has it. It allows you to perceive others' motives, treat them the way they want to be treated, mind their needs, understand how others perceive you, and so on.

It Is Good for Business and Career. Whether you are a business owner or an employee, whether you work in sales or IT, empathy can make all the difference in the world for your career prospects. Good business relationships are built on trust, and to build up trust you have to first understand what the other party wants, needs and expects. Empathy makes this a natural process. Thus, whether you want to build healthy cooperation with your colleagues, employees, and bosses or try to organize trust-based marketing approach, empathy is going to be of great help.

It Lets You Better Understand Non-Verbal Components of Communication. Communication is so much more than what words express. People who are weak at empathy have very hard time reading between the lines of their conversations and understanding that what the other person means, or wants, to communicate to them is something completely different from what they actually say.

It Makes You Be Better at Handling Conflicts. When you subliminally perceive what the other party wants and needs and can understand exactly why they want and need it, reaching a "win-win" solution gets so much easier. You no longer have to blindly grasp for a solution, misreading the other party's signals and searching for a way out in the wrong place.

It Makes It Easier to Convince and Motivate Others. When you are able to see the world from another's point of view, see their motives, feelings, and preconceptions, finding ways to convince others to your point of view and motivating them to do something becomes much easier than when you try to use a one-size-fits-all approach. Different people are motivated by vastly different things, and having empathy means having keys to understanding them on the fly.

It Broadens Your Horizons. If empathy means co-experiencing the world from another person's point of view, feeling with that person, it naturally follows that if you are strong at empathy, it allows you to perceive the world from multiple viewpoints. When you see the world not only from your own perspective, but from the perspectives of other people as well, it lets you perceive it to a fuller extent, see unexpected and previously unknown parts of it and, in general, live a more fulfilled life.

Empathy, on a very basic level, is what makes us human. Thus it is hardly surprising that achieving higher levels of empathy very often means achieving greater success and fulfillment as human beings – which means that concentrating on training your empathetic ability is a very sound course of action.

Empathy is not complex, but it's not easy.

Why is it so scarce and so difficult?

It's threatening. If I truly seek to understand another's point of view, I might discover my closely held position is limited or exposed. And I might even be challenged to change my thinking.

It's emotional. Perhaps even more scary than an unwanted perspective is an unwanted feeling. As I put myself in that other person's shoes, it may feel unfamiliar and uncomfortable. And I might feel some of what the other person is feeling. When I experience strong emotions, the last thing I want to do is seek to understand. Physiologically, my body goes into self-protection mode, and social skills are even more difficult.

It's humbling. If I am genuinely empathetic, not only is it possible that I am reminded that I don't know everything, I might also learn that another person is not as crazy, stupid, wrong or mean as I had made them out to be. And to the extent I was boosting myself up by putting them down, I may fall down a notch or two.

Demonstrating empathy takes effort and practice.

To demonstrate empathy, most of us need to be continually reminded of these tips from Captain Obvious:

Talk less, listen more. If you tend to talk a lot, shoot to listen 70% of the time in each conversation. Come to the conversation prepared with key questions versus statements.

Listen to connect. Listening for information and listening to solve problems can be better than not listening at all, but they don't necessarily build trusting relationships. Actively listening with empathy is a powerful and conversationally intelligent approach.

Let the other person go first. This is especially tough when you have a strong point of view. But when you've done your best to hear and put yourself in the other person's shoes first, you will be more effective in stating your view in an empathetic way when it's your turn.

Let people know you understand before moving on. Discipline yourself to take the 'extra' step of restating, paraphrasing or somehow confirming that you heard and understand them before they move to the next topic or before you explain yourself. This slows the conversation down, but it can help lower the temperature if it's too heated and will likely save time in the long run.

Opportunities to practice empathy abound. All we have to do is look on the news, across the aisle, or across the hall. Where is your next opportunity to demonstrate empathy?

CHAPTER 12

TALKING WITH ANYONE

You're at a party or a conference or just walking along the street when you see someone you would like to talk with. It might be someone you've admired from afar, someone who might be a good customer or investor for your company or someone you simply like the looks of. You struggle for the right thing to say that would get the two of you talking, but before you can come up with anything good, the person has moved on or gotten involved in a different conversation and the moment has passed.

If this has happened to you, it needn't ever happen again. You can gracefully start a conversation with absolutely anyone, anytime. There's only one secret: Say something the person will be happy to hear. With that in mind, it should be very clear that a political comment (unless you really know the listener's politics), anything that could be seen as offensive, and most complaining is off the table. So is any kind of gossip.

Instead, walk up to the person, speak pleasantly, and pick the most appropriate of the conversation-starters below. There's a decent chance you'll be chatting away in no time. At the very least, you'll likely be able to get contact info you can use later on.

Make Note Of Something Pleasant. "This dip is delicious!" "Nice turnout for this event!" "Did you hear the keynote? I thought it was great." There's something positive to say in nearly every situation, so find it and say it. Don't say something negative because it's much too risky. "I thought the keynote was boring," could backfire if the listener turns out to be the keynote speaker's cousin.

Comment On The Weather. The one exception to the no-negatives rule is weather. If you're in the midst of a heat wave, cold snap, or torrential downpour, remarking on the unusual weather is often a good way to start a conversation -- it's a shared experience, one that both you and the listener are having. If it's a particularly lovely day, that's a good way to start too.

Ask For Information. "Excuse me, do you know what time the next session starts?" Even if you already know the answer, asking for information can be a great way to start someone talking with you, because everyone likes to feel helpful.

Ask For Assistance. "Could you reach that item on the top shelf for me?" "I dropped my ring and I think it rolled under your table. Would you take a quick look?" Requests for assistance are another way to make someone feel helpful. Just make sure whatever you ask for is something the listener can provide without much inconvenience.

Offer Assistance. You won't often find yourself in a situation where you can help someone you're dying to talk to, but if it happens, don't miss your chance to be of use. "Can I help you carry that large box?" "Do you need a seat? There's a free one over here." "Would you like a program? I happen to have an extra." The listener will be inclined to like you and trust you because you've helped out. Be careful not to be intrusive or excessive. "I couldn't help overhearing that your credit card was declined -- would you like to use mine?" will do more harm than good.

Solicit An Opinion. "What did you think of that speech?" "Did you get a lot out of this workshop?" "I see you're drinking the special cocktail. Would you recommend it?" Most people like knowing that others are interested in their opinions and will be happy to respond.

Mention A Mutual Acquaintance. "Did you used to work with Roger? He and I have done several projects together." Naming someone you both know will tell the listener you are part of his or her extended social circle. Many people will begin thinking of you as someone they know or should know. Be careful, though, that their relationship with your shared acquaintance is on good terms -- you don't want to say you're best friends with someone only to learn your friend and the listener are in the midst of a legal dispute.

Bring Up A Shared Experience. Does the listener come from the same town or region as you? Did you attend the same high school or college? Have you both worked for the same company or boss? Do you both love to scuba dive? Any common ground is a good way to start someone talking, especially if you use it as a reason to ask for information or advice. "Do you know what happened to John who used to work there?" "Do you prefer warm-water or cold-water diving?"

Praise The Listener. This works when you're wondering what to say to a celebrity, a noted VC, or someone prominent in your industry or company. You'll never insult someone by saying, "I really love your work," or "I thought your last blog post was very insightful." Three caveats: Don't fawn, don't make the mistake of critiquing the listener, as in "I thought your most recent movie was much better than last year's." And only offer praise if you genuinely mean it.

Compliment The Listener's Apparel Or Accessories.
"That's a really unusual necktie. Where did you get it?"
"That scarf is a great color on you." Most people like it
when others appreciate their taste, so they will likely
want to engage with you. Don't comment on the
listener's own physical appearance -- having a stranger
or near-stranger tell you that you have beautiful eyes is
more creepy than anything else. The exception is hair. If
the listener has recently changed hairstyle or had a
haircut, it's fine to compliment that. (But if someone
started coloring hair to remove the grey, best to keep
that comment to yourself.)

Simply Introduce Yourself. This won't work in every
setting but in many cases, if you truly can't come up
with an appealing conversational gambit, you can try
the direct approach. Walk up to the person, stick out
your hand and say, "Hi, I'm so-and-so. I just wanted to
introduce myself." The fact that you went out of your
way to meet will make the listener feel important. It will
probably make the person want to talk to you, as well.

CHAPTER 13

DARK CONVERSATION, HOW TO CONVINCE ANYONE

The ability to persuade is crucial in the business world. On a day-to-day basis, you need it to convince employees to work toward company goals or to persuade colleagues or clients to consider your ideas and suggestions. If you can master the art of persuasive communication, you can win the support of others, unify your team and encourage them to work together.

If you're looking for new ways to persuade people, just read on and learn how to become a master at the art of persuasion. First, I want to clarify that persuasion is not manipulation because while manipulation is coercion through force to make someone do something they don't want to do, persuasion "is the art of getting people to do things that are in their own best interest that also benefit you." There are a lot of resources available online that can help you master this skill, you just have to be willing to put a bit of effort into it and to have enough patience. It's extremely important to develop this skill since it will help you get ahead in business and personal relationships. Most influential people on this planet, whether they are political leaders or important social figures, are incredibly persuasive. You can be this way too if you just pay attention to these next very efficient ways to persuade anyone to do anything easily:

Know Your Audience. How you craft your message will depend on whether you're sending a memo to your staff or giving a presentation to the entire company. Effective persuasive communication addresses the audience's needs, values, and desires. Audiences respond better to persuasive communication when they feel the person speaking is similar to them in some way, whether it's in age, occupation or socio-economic status. If you address what's important to your audience, they'll see you as someone who is similar to them. Therefore, they should be more receptive to your message, too.

Establish Credibility. To persuade an audience, you must demonstrate your credibility and authority.

People are more receptive to someone they view as an authority figure, whether that person has direct authority over them, such as a boss, or if the person is an authority in his industry or profession. You should attempt to persuade others of something you can prove or have first-hand knowledge of or experience in. Back up your claims with statistics or examples.

Before you can persuade an audience, you must first grab their attention and demonstrate why it's worth their time to listen to your idea or suggestion. Start with an anecdote that illustrates the point you're trying to make or with a surprising fact that tells them why what you have to say is important. For example, if you're trying to persuade company management to adopt a no-smoking policy, begin with a statistic regarding how many sick days smokers take compared to non-smokers.

Tailor the Message to the Medium. What persuades in writing doesn't necessarily persuade when delivered verbally. For example, you can include numbers and statistics in a written document because readers can take their time interpreting the data. But if you bombard listeners with these same figures during a speech, you may confuse them and lose their attention. Face-to-face interaction often is more effective at persuading others because you can create a personal connection with your audience and use eye contact, gestures and other nonverbal signals to maintain their attention.

Convey Benefits. It's easier to persuade an audience when you can show them how your proposal benefits them. If you're asking your staff to work overtime during a busy season, describe how the extra money generated will fund additional employee perks or physical improvements to the workplace. If you're trying to convince your supervisor to let you work from home part time, mention studies illustrating that employees are more productive when allowed to telecommute. If you're pitching an idea to a client, explain how using your idea will improve the company's image and attract more customers.

Use Body Language. With verbal communication, your demeanor influences your ability to persuade as much as your words. If you cross your arms, your audience may perceive you as hostile or angry. If you fidget, they may see you as weak or uncertain. If you rarely make eye contact, they may think you're hiding something. To sell your message to your audience, connect with them by maintaining eye contact. Project authority and confidence by standing up straight. Demonstrate your sincerity and openness by relaxing your arms and keeping them at your sides – unless you're using them to gesture – instead of crossing them behind or in front of you.

Focus On How You Can Be Helpful. I call this the "service mentality." When your goal is to convince or persuade someone, don't focus on how you can get them to do something. Instead, focus on how you can be helpful. Think about what the other person's goals and objectives are and how you can help get them there.

Provide Context. Having the desire to help is the first step, but you'll also need to give some context to demonstrate that your ideas can work. If you're presenting a new idea to your boss, for example, come prepared with a detailed business case, competitive intelligence, research, other people's opinions, and any other insight you can leverage.

Expect Resistance - And Plan How You'll Move Past It. In any exchange of information, you should prepare to be met with resistance. I'm talking about that N-O word. The natural reaction is to shut down. But so often resistance can be an opportunity to move the exchange to the next level of engagement. Understanding concerns, objections, and barriers is critical to making forward progress. Great sellers view resistance as an opportunity to learn, understand and advance the dialogue. Which leads us to...

Ask Intelligent, Open-Ended Questions. Asking good questions is one of the most important ways to communicate more successfully. When you are met with resistance, probe. Go deep enough so that you walk away from the conversation with new information and insight (instead of walking away empty-handed and frustrated). Learn more - their position, challenges, needs and areas of confusion - so that you can help them move beyond their resistance and into their comfort zone. Show up prepared with intelligent questions. Being prepared for tough conversations beats winging it every time.

Goals of a Persuasive Speech: Convincing, Actuation, and/or Stimulation

The overall goal of a persuasive speech is for the audience to accept your viewpoint as the speaker. However, this is not a nuanced enough definition to capture the actual goals of different persuasive speeches. Persuasive speeches can be designed to convince, actuate, and/or stimulate the audience.

Convincing. A convincing speech is designed to cause the audience to internalize and believe a viewpoint that they did not previously hold. In a sense, a convincing argument changes the audience's mind. For example, suppose you are giving a persuasive speech claiming that Coke is better than Pepsi. Your goal is not just for the audience to hear that you enjoy Coke more, but for Pepsi lovers to change their minds.

Actuation. An actuation speech has a slightly different goal. An actuation speech is designed to cause the audience to do something, to take some action. This type of speech is particularly useful if the audience already shares some or all of your view. For example, at the end of presidential campaigns, candidates begin to focus on convincing their supporters to actually vote. They are seeking to actuate the action of voting through their speeches.

Stimulation. Persuasive speeches can also be used to enhance how fervently the audience believes in an idea. In this instance, the speaker understands that the audience already believes in the viewpoint, but not to the degree that he or she would like. As a result, the speaker tries to stimulate the audience, making them more enthusiastic about the view. For example, religious services often utilize stimulation. They are not trying to convince those of another religion to switch religions necessarily; there is an understanding that the congregation already accepts part or all of the religion. Instead, they are trying to enhance the degree of belief.

CHAPTER 14

THE IMPORTANCE OF CONSCIOUS COMMUNICATION

Our communication with the environment begins in the mother's womb: we react to stimuli, although these responses are not thought out. As we grow, our communication is designed, practised and modified to respond to certain social standards. So, there comes a time when we can talk about intentional communication and conscious communication.

The communication of our needs facilitates survival, establishing links with the people around us. It is something natural that arises spontaneously in us. However, recently much has been said about another type of communication: conscious communication.

Being aware of the present moment is what mindfulness, mindfulness or conscious communication gives us. In a world like the present, where our way of communicating with the environment is multiple, there are studies that recommend that we focus on one task at a time, facing the modern temptation to work in multitasking mode or with divided attention. This includes both producing and receiving information. To communicate is not only to produce information but also to know how to interpret it.

What is mindfulness?

We often know what we say, we firmly believe in our point of view, but we share our attention when we receive messages. So, let's reflect: do we really listen or pay no attention to what the other says, simply wanting to recover the word? Are we aware of our non-verbal communication? For better or for worse, it conveys much of the messages we communicate.

Being a conscious communicator is just that: participating in all of our communication. And it is not an easy process; it is necessary to start in schools, where some exercises related to conscious communication are already practised. For example, the exercises in empathy and acceptance of the other are a good way to introduce this topic to children. Emotions are fundamental in our day to day and mastering them requires a lot of patience and practice, although sometimes we forget that.

Being aware or aware involves not giving in to irritation or anger in communicating with others. Knowing when to let go of emotions is a sign of conscious communication and, in this task, emotional intelligence will help us. Emotional intelligence manifests itself in the domain of our emotions, as well as in the acceptance of the emotions of others.

How to practice conscious communication?

The first step to follow when we want to be conscious communicators is to understand that communication is a process. Wanting to be attentive or aware does not mean being like that. This skill covers many areas:

- Spelling and good dialectic. A person who makes spelling mistakes, who bases his language on crutches or does not structure his speech correctly is a communicator who harms his own communication. The word is one of our first cover letters, so speaking correctly is always a good idea.

- The lack of emotions in the speech. Communication is not based solely on the transmission of information; if we only produce information, it will be more difficult to reach the recipients of the message. If we speak with emotion, we will gain the attention and empathy of others. The effect will be immediate: the public will feel part of the communicative process, we will have your involvement, your attention. It also increases the likelihood that our message will be recorded in your memory.

- Non-verbal communication. Non-verbal communication refers not only to gestures and other types of body language, but also to the implicit or pragmatic information that we share with our interlocutor. Therefore, we will try to take care of both aspects: it is important that our body language indicates that we are open to dialogue and other ways of thinking. In addition, pragmatic elements are essential. The language or the implicit emotions, the social codes that we share or reject, must be continually in our minds to get along with the people with whom we communicate.

- Responsibility towards feelings. Not everyone feels the same way, so we don't express our emotions equally. If we want something from others, we must find the most appropriate way to ask for what we want.

Being a conscious communicator makes us more efficient, more empathetic communicators, and allows us to express ourselves in a way that is more adapted to our social context and create stronger social bonds. We are talking about a difficult process, because it will involve, among other achievements, identifying and recognizing our current mistakes, but it will also be worth reaping the rewards.

CHAPTER 15

THE IMPORTANCE OF EMOTIONAL COMMUNICATION

Several researches on natural creation and attachment have shown the importance of physical contact since birth.

Caresses and hugs have a special power, the power to communicate affections and feelings, which from birth the baby knows how to understand, receive and internalize.

That is why, in many hospitals, the skin-to-skin act of the mother with her baby is practiced from the very moment of birth. , to provoke the mammalian nature of attachment and the recognition of its main reference.

Communication without interference

There are several ways of communicating, on the one hand verbal communication, which is transmitted through words, and non-verbal communication, that which is expressed through gestures, postures, tone of voice, timbre, etc...

In addition, we could say that there is another way of communicating, emotional communication, one that transmits emotions, feelings and desires, and without a doubt, this happens through physical contact.

In our culture, as in so many others, kissing is used as part of the cordial greeting between two people known or not, and this social protocol has caused the loss of the affective component that it has in essence.

However, kissing a loved one, or your spouse, recovers the affective component that is expressed on the most intimate level.

The caresses also get emotional and sensual sense in the most intimate and private plan, with an emotional language in themselves.

And hugs are the only gesture that has transcended the social and public plan, preserving the affective and expression of desires component.

Personal zones

In interpersonal relationships there are several spaces or zones in which we can interact.

First of all, the public area, where you interact with several people at the same time, for example, when we present a lecture and we are at a distance of approximately 3.5 to 7m.

On the other hand, there is the social zone in which we interact with one or two unknown people, approximately 1.20 to 3.50m away.

Then there is the personal zone 1, which is the distance to reach out or hold a public conversation, approximately between 45cm and 1.20m.

And finally, the intimate zone, which few people access, since it is a zone reserved for people from the most intimate level, in which interactions are based on physical contact, at distances of 45 cm or less.

It is in this intimate space that the different options for emotional communication emerge through physical contact, sometimes on a social and public plane, other times on a private plane, as in love relationships.

But without a doubt, maintaining physical contact is entering the intimate area, in which the person is most vulnerable, and where the intrusion of a person to whom we have not given access will make us feel invaded, attacked or little respected.

It is precisely for fear that this will happen that we put up barriers that prevent access to any person not chosen for this, relegating them to the personal zone, absent from physical contact.

Physical contact, source of knowledge and empathy

Emotional communication through physical contact has a strong potential for interpersonal relationships, as it helps us to feel more about the other person, practicing empathy and respect in relation to their emotions and feelings more naturally.

Opening our intimate area more often will allow us to know the most sensitive, emotional and human plan of people, then breaking barriers or masks that sometimes prevent us from understanding, respecting or feeling loved.

Living the experience of physical contact with receptive people for this deepens the meaning of life and human relationships.

For a simple gesture, without words, allows us to feel much more than a speech, and therefore, in just an instant we will understand that we are part of that person's life and that we are not alone.

CONCLUSION

People spend a large part of our time communicating verbally. Also through bodily expressions such as the movement of the hands, the distances that people keep from each other, etc.

Example: the man arrives very early at his office and reviews his correspondence (written communication), then his secretary enters, whom he greets with a nod (gestural communication). At noon, after a phone call (spoken communication) he goes to a meeting with his partners (group communication). So on, the man constantly communicates with all his surroundings.

Outside of this type of denomination, communication is a large industry in which many people participate respecting their roles. According to many researchers, currently it has imposed the tendency to manipulate symbols and not things like the time of our grandparents. The industry is not only interested in the quality of its product, but in the "impact" it produces.

Scientific research has given rise to new professions such as science popularizer and technical writer to be able to quickly "communicate" recent advances.

Many years ago, communication did not disturb the attention of large governments, the technological and philosophical revolution changed the course of this trend, therefore, government agencies began to place special emphasis on "communication" as a method of survival in the face of concerns. worldwide.

If we want to maintain a directive position in the world we have to understand others and make them understand us.

Our basic objective in communication is to become effective agents, that is, to influence others, the physical world that surrounds us and ourselves, in such a way that we can become determining agents and feel capable, if necessary, of taking decisions. In short, we communicate to influence and to affect intentionally.

Whoever tries to report has the purpose of transmitting an accumulation of data to a receiver, regardless of the recipient's response (weather reports, decisions of a boss, instructions from a manual). Whoever tries to persuade wants to obtain a certain response, through a communicational process in which the other also obtain what they want or what they "think" they want.

In this process, active in both directions, the roles of persuader and persuaded are often easily swapped. Persuasion is not something you "do to" others, but rather a dynamic that takes place with others. Therefore, persuasive communication only takes place to the extent that the feedback obtained is as expected, otherwise, there was no communication but only an exchange of information took place.

In short, it is the response of the recipient that qualifies the nature of the transaction.

Examples:

A seller who dispels the doubts of his client, circumvents his objectives and manages to place his product, is an example of persuasive communication, since the buyer receives satisfaction in return based on their needs, tastes or preferences. If he had not been able to save his client's questions, there would only have been an information crossing.

Whoever tries to entertain pursues a recreational purpose. It seeks to maintain the attention and pleasure principle of the recipient throughout the transaction. This type of communication has an end that seeks to be consummated. No response is expected beyond approval (a TV show, shows, etc.).

Then some questions arise such as: Why communications? What is our object? The basic aim of every individual is to dominate the environment that surrounds him and not for the environment to dominate him.

Another question is: What is the answer that the issuer is trying to obtain? We can affirm that all communication has its objective, which is to produce a response. The purpose of communication is often confused, and this is because man, as the greatest exponent of communication, sometimes does not know well what his purpose is. What is suggested in the face of this fact is to focus attention on the purpose of communication in order to achieve a goal as communicators. On the contrary, the purpose of the communication would be lost, since the message would not achieve significance.

Communication failure can be attributed to the following causes: lack of efficiency or misinterpretation.